I'm a Christian
so what do I believe?

Ken Gardiner

instant
apostle

First published in Great Britain in 2013

Instant Apostle
The Hub
3-5 Rickmansworth Road
Watford
Herts
WD18 OGX

British Library Cataloguing-in-Publication Data

A catalogue record for this book is available from the British Library

This book and all other Instant Apostle books are available from Instant Apostle:

Website: www.instantapostle.com
E-mail: info@instantapostle.com

ISBN 978-0-9559135-9-4

Printed in Great Britain

Instant Apostle is a new way of getting ideas flowing, between followers of Jesus, and between those who would like to know more about His Kingdom.

It's not just about books and it's not about a one-way information flow. It's about building a community where ideas are exchanged. Ideas will be expressed at an appropriate length. Some will take the form of books. But in many cases ideas can be expressed more briefly than in a book. Short books, or pamphlets, will be an important part of what we provide. As with pamphlets of old, these are likely to be opinionated, and produced quickly so that the community can discuss them.

Well-known authors are welcome, but we also welcome new writers. We are looking for prophetic voices, authentic and original ideas, produced at any length; quick and relevant, insightful and opinionated. And as the name implies, these will be released very quickly, either as Kindle books or printed texts or both.

Join the community. Get reading, get writing and get discussing!

Contents

Foreword..9

Where I am..11

Chapter 1 What am I for? 13

Chapter 2 The Law 29

Chapter 3 The Bible (1)..49

Chapter 4 The Bible (2)..69

Chapter 5 Jesus..85

Chapter 6 What happens now?.................................112

Chapter 7 What happens then?.................................135

Chapter 8 My Lord and my God 162

Foreword

Ken Gardiner is your man, really. If I were to ask for a guide as to what we believe as Christians and what this means in practice, I would trust my life with Ken's explanation.

In a culture which has a broken Christian memory and which seems unable to put its fractured pieces back together in a way that makes sense of the whole, Ken's apologetic is invaluable. This is a patient, involved, wise interpretation of the Christian story. He does not patronise or take anything for granted in the reader and explains in a logical, intelligible way how the story of God's encounter with the human race began and found its culmination in the life, sacrifice and resurrection of Jesus Christ.

In doing so, Ken draws on a lifetime's experience of faith and ministry; he was ordained 50 years ago and still retains a passion for debating and sharing what Christians believe. His final chapter is an intimate account of his own story and the grace of God, ensuring that the book is clearly rooted in a personal rather than an abstract view of faith. His intention is that readers might join him on this road and be strengthened by a deeper appreciation of God, Jesus, the Bible, the Holy Spirit, the Church and the world to come.

As someone who knows him and listens to what other people say about him, Ken can be trusted by the reader as a man who has walked the walk as much as this book shows he can talk the talk! I have a feeling some people are going to have their lives changed through the reading of it.

The Venerable Simon Burton-Jones
Archdeacon of Rochester

Where I am

For many people today, it seems that life is like a ride on a roller coaster. They certainly travel and they experience its highs and lows, but at the end they haven't actually gone anywhere; they get off where they got on.

I am a Christian and so I believe that I am on a journey, and it is a journey towards God. Over the years, my understanding of Him has developed; some of the things I was taught when I was young I have amended, and even rejected, and there are many truths I have discovered for myself – only to realise later that others had discovered them ahead of me. My experience has been so rich that I want to share what I can in the hope that it will help and encourage others on their own journeys.

This is not a book of Christian doctrine but, because it explains what I believe, it does set out many basic truths of the Christian faith. I am aware that some of my ideas are controversial; however, I quote the Scriptural texts which have led me to my conclusions and I firmly believe they are not heretical even if, in some cases, they represent a minority view.

We are all different and so we have different ways of looking at things, as well as different needs, and I believe that God relates to each of us individually. Therefore my experiences of Him will not be exactly the same as yours. Nevertheless, we will have much in common, and my thoughts may prompt you to explore new ideas for yourself.

A friend suggested that I should include a bibliography of the books which have helped me in my understanding. I have found this impossible to compile because I cannot recall where I first learned this or that, and, anyway, the original idea has now become so much a part of my own thinking and development that almost certainly it no longer reflects exactly what the author originally wrote. I can only acknowledge my debt to countless writers, teachers and preachers who have helped me on my way but who must remain anonymous.

Please allow me to clarify at the outset one possible cause of offence: to avoid unnecessary complication, I refer throughout to God as 'He', but this carries no connotation of gender. All that we are, male and female, springs equally from Him.

Ken Gardiner can be contacted on his website: www.kengardiner.co.uk

Chapter 1
What am I for?

It all depends on whether or not there is a creator. If there is not, then this universe, and indeed every other universe there may be, is simply a chance happening and so there is no meaning and no purpose to anything. To ask 'What am I for?' is futile; we are not *for* anything. For many people, however, there is too much design in the created order for it just to have 'happened': design requires a designer, an intelligence. St Paul uses this argument in his letter to the Romans:

> Since what may be known about God is plain to them, because God has made it plain to them. For since the creation of the world God's invisible qualities – his eternal power and divine nature – have been clearly seen, being understood from what has been made.
> *Romans 1:19-20*

In fact, Paul has extended the argument beyond the revelation that there is a creator; he claims that it reveals much about what that creator is like. However, this reasoning is not definitive because it simply puts the problem one stage back. Sooner or later – and as very young children raise this question it is probably sooner – we are bound to ask, 'Well, if God made the world, who made God?' All the potential of creation must, obviously, be contained within its creator before he creates. So to say that creation presupposes that there is a creator does not prove that God exists but, equally, it does not prove that He does not. It is a matter of faith. We may not be able to reason ourselves to a position of faith (if we could, it wouldn't be faith; it would have become factual knowledge), but faith is not unreasonable. If you think about it, that is only fair. If belief in God were to depend upon intelligence – an ability to reason it out – then clever people would have an advantage. On the other hand, if faith was so unreasonable that anyone with a grain of intelligence could see that it was impossible, only dimwits would believe. No, faith must belong to a different sphere from reason – even though we will need to exercise reason within that faith once we have it. The writer of the letter to the Hebrews explains how God is to be found:

> Without faith it is impossible to please God, because anyone who comes to him must believe that he exists and that he rewards those who earnestly seek him.
> *Hebrews 11:6*

The reward, of course, is finding what is sought. Some people, scientists in particular, may claim that it is unreasonable to demand that you have to believe that God exists before you can discover that He does; but, in fact, this approach is one that scientists themselves adopt in making their discoveries. As I write, scientists using the Large Hadron Collider at Cern in Switzerland are searching for the Higgs boson particle (the so-called 'God' particle) because discoveries already made predict that it exists. That is to say, their belief that it exists encourages them to search for it in the expectation that their search will prove successful – exactly what the above quotation is asking of us if we would find God. However, there is a major difference in the type of truth that is discovered.

Science demands physical or material proof that can be visibly demonstrated, but there is another sphere of truth which does not operate in that way. Perhaps the most obvious example is the appreciation of beauty; a painting, a piece of music or a poem may be regarded as beautiful and, even allowing that tastes may differ and that beauty lies in the eyes of the beholder, there *is* such a thing as experiencing beauty.

To quote another example, I remember witnessing a discussion between two men when one had mentioned his joy that he had a wife who loved him. The other decided to play devil's advocate and claimed that he could not know that. The first recited a list of kind deeds which his wife had performed towards him and the other said that she had done this because she wanted to keep him sweet because he was the breadwinner and provided a home and an income which allowed her to indulge her hobbies and gave her time to meet up with friends, etc. The argument went to and fro until, in exasperation, the husband declared, 'I just *know* she loves me!'

Day by day, we all make decisions based on beliefs we hold which cannot be proved scientifically to be right. I appreciate how frustrating it must be to someone who cannot accept as true anything that cannot be factually demonstrated, but I can say only that I know God. My challenger may argue that I cannot be so sure, that my certainty is based on feelings which can be prompted by all sorts of conditions – medical, mental, psychological, temperamental and by my upbringing. To this I must respond, 'I know what I know and I have staked my life on it,' which, of course, he will find even more infuriating. However, I would point out that if he is an atheist he, also, is staking his life on what he believes but cannot prove – that there is no God.

Whatever arguments may be advanced for the existence of God, they will not be definitive for everyone, and so the Bible presents no such arguments. Its opening words proclaim simply, 'In the beginning God...' (Genesis 1:1). (Yes, I know I have stopped in mid sentence: it continues, '...created the heavens and the earth', but it still makes the point that God existed and then He created all that is.)

If the question, 'Who made God?' could be answered, the next would be, 'Then who made who made God?' When you have taken all those questions back and back to what first existed then, the Christian faith claims, 'That is what we mean by God.' To claim that what first existed was the Higgs boson particle, or its predecessors, is no more believable than to say 'God', because the same question arises: 'Who made the particle?' Recently, scientists have claimed that the created order does not require anything or anyone to have created it; the Christian would say the same about God.

John's Gospel echoes the opening words of Genesis but enhances their truth:

> In the beginning was the Word, and the Word was with God, and the Word was God.
> *John 1:1*

John is writing after the earthly ministry of Jesus and His death and resurrection and, in the light of that, he claims that Christ existed before God began the work of creation; indeed, He was not only *with* God but *is Himself* God. John refers to Him as 'the Word'. What is a word? It is a means of self-expression. I have ideas in my mind which I want to share with you, so I put those ideas into words which you hear or read and hopefully understand sufficiently in order to grasp the ideas I am seeking to convey. J. B. Phillips in his translation actually describes Jesus as God's personal expression.

Jesus is the most perfect expression of God that mankind has ever been given, although creation itself is an expression of God; indeed, God continues to express Himself, as we are told in the letter to the Hebrews:

> The Son is the radiance of God's glory and the exact representation of his being, sustaining all things by his powerful word.
> *Hebrews 1:3*

(I prefer the old King James translation which says, 'by the word of his power' – i.e., by the expression of His power.)

John records Jesus as saying, 'My Father is always at his work to this very day, and I too am working' (John 5:17). God is constantly expressing Himself; restoring, redeeming, upholding, healing and guiding, in the furtherance of His plan. It is important that we understand what His plan is because only then can we discover our part in it and learn what we have been created for. To do that we need to understand a little more about God.

The Trinity

Christians believe that what we call God is not just one person but three. When I was young I was told to think of a shamrock with its three leaves as a helpful illustration of how that could be. I duly thought of it but I didn't find it at all helpful; simply confusing.

I once heard a preacher attempt an explanation by saying that as a person he fulfilled three roles: he was a son to his parents, a husband to his wife and a father to his children. A similar explanation is that water can take three modes: ice, liquid and steam. These two illustrations are actually a heresy known as 'modalism', and they turn the doctrine of the Trinity on its head. The first takes one person expressing himself in three modes or roles, whereas the truth of the Trinity is that it is three persons expressing themselves in one mode – God. The same error relates to the one substance of water expressing itself in three modes.

I find it more helpful to think of a choir. How many choirs are there? One! How many people are in it? Several. Are they all singing the same thing? Well, hopefully they are all singing the same piece of music but, no, they are singing different notes; there are sopranos, contraltos, tenors and basses, but they blend together in perfect harmony.

Perhaps I should speak of a trio of piano, violin and cello, as this involves only three performers – an illustration which conforms more closely to the truth of the Trinity; but you understand the illustration. There is the Father, the Son and the Holy Spirit. Each has a particular role to fulfil but they work together in perfect harmony. There are not three Gods any more than there are three choirs or trios. There are three persons; each is equally God but, nevertheless, there is a sense in which the Father is the superior.

Paul, writing to the Philippians, gives some interesting information about the Father's response to the obedience of His Son in dying on the cross:

Therefore God exalted him to the highest place and gave him the name that is above every name, that at the name of Jesus every knee should bow, in heaven and on earth and under the earth, and every tongue confess that Jesus Christ is Lord, to the glory of God the Father.
Philippians 2:9-11

That is not implying that until then Jesus was not God, but it does state that He was exalted. Let's look at it like this: Prince Charles, eldest son of the Queen and Prince Philip, was born on 14th November 1948. From that moment he was royalty – he had 'blue blood', as they say. He was no less 'royal' than his mother but, as Queen, she was superior to him. He was invested as Prince of Wales by the Queen on 1st July 1969 at Caernarfon Castle. He was given a title he did not have previously but it did not make him more royal. We must not take this illustration too literally as a description of the relationship between the Father and the Son, but it may help in our understanding of their roles within the Trinity we know as 'God'.

The Holy Spirit also has His role; He interprets God's thoughts and expresses them (1 Corinthians 2:9-16) and He brings glory to the Son (John 16:14). He is self-effacing but He is much more than simply an influence. Paul instructs us not to grieve the Holy Spirit and so, if He can be grieved, He must be a person with what we know as emotions. Whilst Scripture does not speak of the Holy Spirit actually expressing His own love, surely He does more than convey the love of the Father and the Son. If He is a person with emotions then He can and does love. The alternative is to say that He has the ability to love the Father and the Son but does not actually do so, which is unthinkable.

Scripture tells us that 'God is love' (1 John 4:8). Notice that it does not say that 'God *has* love', because that would imply that He exists anyway (with or without love) and one of the attributes He has is love. No, love is what He *is* in His very essence. The Father loves the Son and the Spirit, the Son loves the Spirit and the Father and the Spirit loves the Father and the Son. This love flowing between them is so great and builds up more and more until it explodes (with a big bang?), expressed in the words, 'Let us make mankind in our image, in our likeness' (Genesis 1:26) – that is, 'Let's expand this love which we are; let's create someone else we can love and who will love us in return.'

We must not fall into the trap of thinking that God *needed* to create humankind; the doctrine of the Trinity illustrates the truth that God is self-sufficient, because each person of the Godhead has the other two to love and to be loved by in return. So God did not *need* to create someone else to love (if God were ever to need anything, He would be less than perfect until that need was met); rather, it is the nature of love to increase, to create. It isn't just fortuitous that we refer to the human act of procreation as 'making love'.

So here we have the first indication of what we are for and why we exist – God (Father, Son and Holy Spirit) desired

19

someone else to share in His love. We were loved into existence and we are to express love ourselves.

It is not surprising, therefore, that on the last night that Jesus spent with His disciples, after Judas had left to betray Him to the priests and knowing that He had very little time to give them final instructions, He said:

> My children, I will be with you only a little longer. You will look for me, and just as I told the Jews, so I tell you now: Where I am going, you cannot come. A new command I give you: Love one another. As I have loved you, so you must love one another. By this all men will know that you are my disciples, if you love one another.
> *John 13:33-35*

His own witness to the truth was about to come to an end because He was leaving the world and returning to the Father, but the disciples would remain and continue the witness. And what would reveal the nature of God most clearly to the world was to reflect the image in which they and all mankind were made – love, because God is love.

Our two basic needs

The deepest need of every human being is to be loved – to know that we matter to at least somebody. There are people who, as children, have been failed by those who should have shown them love, and instead they have experienced rejection. It hurts so much to desire love and for that desire not to be met that their only defence is to shut down the desire. As adults, they do not dare to open up that desire, for that would make them vulnerable to the pain all over again. Unfortunately, this applies to their dealings not only with other human beings but also with God, and they never experience the joy of the relationship for which they were created. One of the greatest rewards of my ministry has been to draw alongside such people and share with them the truth of a statement in Paul's letter to the Ephesians:

For he [the Father] chose us in him [Jesus] before the creation of the world to be holy and blameless in his sight. *Ephesians 1:4*

I remember speaking with a young woman in the depth of depression who had been told by her mother that she hadn't been wanted and that she, the mother, had only married her father because she was pregnant. I explained that even before He had created anything, God knew that there would be a time when He wanted someone else to love, and He had chosen to create *her* for that purpose. Maybe her parents hadn't wanted her, but God did, and He had used her parents' act of procreation to bring her into being. I have never forgotten her wonder as she asked, 'Is that true; is it really true?'

We all exist because God desired someone else to love and to love Him in return. That reciprocal need that we have, to give love as well as to receive it, is illustrated even in young children who will cuddle and speak to teddy bears and dolls. Adults may have dogs and cats to care for and love; indeed, some who find it difficult to relate to other human beings will often donate large sums in their wills to animal rescue charities because the love they need to express is directed towards animals, who are less likely to reject or abuse that love than other human beings.

Although the desire for love may be our primary need, there is another which runs it fairly close – the need to achieve: we all want to be good at something. I well remember decorating a room and calling my wife to admire the first few pieces of wallpaper I had managed to hang. Her role was to say, 'Well done, it looks really good,' and I was somewhat annoyed when what she actually said was, 'You have missed a bit under the shelf.'

I have noticed that those who feel that they have not been loved will often compensate by seeking success in what they achieve. It is a sort of, 'You may not love me, but look what I can do. I do matter because I have something to contribute.'

So we were created not only for love but also to achieve something, and God has something for us to do. Having created mankind, God said:

> Be fruitful and increase in number; fill the earth and subdue it. Rule over the fish in the sea and the birds in the sky and over every living creature that moves on the ground.
> *Genesis 1:28*

We human beings have been given the role not only of procreating but also of acting as God's stewards to care for the earth and everything on it. It was intended to be a task of joy and fulfilment.

I believe that most Christians do not appreciate just what God was doing in making us rulers over the earth: He was pledging Himself to work on earth only through the cooperation of mankind. The only exception to this is that occasionally (and certainly not always) He will act in judgment on sin without waiting for us to ask. God's intention was that we should live in such a close relationship with Him that we should consult Him to discover His plans and then work to bring them to fruition. As stewards, we would be entitled to ask Him for whatever we needed to fulfil His purposes.

Although that plan has been thwarted and disrupted by mankind's disobedience (we will deal with that more fully in the next chapter), God has not changed His mind: we still have dominion over the earth and God works on it only through the cooperation of mankind. If we understand this concept, it will do much to curtail the criticism that He does not act to alleviate so much of the pain and suffering in the world today. At the risk of running ahead of myself in what is to come in this book, let me remind you of the time when more than 5,000 people had gathered out in the country to listen to Jesus, and the disciples came to Him in concern that they all needed to be fed. Jesus responded by saying, 'You give them something to eat.' As we look out on a world where so many are starving and we pray to God in our concern for them, I wonder if He is saying the same to us – '*You* give them something to eat.' With the 5,000, Jesus worked a miracle, and He did it not by manufacturing food from thin air but by taking what the people already had and multiplying it. But that involved a young lad giving up the whole of his lunch before receiving back his fair share – what he needed.

This truth that God has limited Himself to work on earth only through the cooperation of mankind is illustrated by a statement in the book of the prophet Ezekiel. God instructs Ezekiel to proclaim what He (God) intends to do. First there will be judgment on Israel's enemies and then there is a long list of blessings He will bestow upon His people. At the end of the list God says, 'Once again I will yield to Israel's plea and do this for them' (Ezekiel 36:37).

Other translations are even more specific, stating that God will allow Israel to ask Him to do it or that He is ready to listen to their prayers for Him to act. That is to say, God shares His plans with His people but waits until they ask Him to bring those plans to fruition, because He has set human beings as the rulers over His earth and will not intervene without our cooperation. This makes sense of His statement in the book of the prophet Isaiah: 'Before they call I will answer; while they are still speaking I will hear' (Isaiah 65:24).

His plans are ready, and only awaiting the first word of our request, so to speak, before He acts. It also explains why Jesus was careful to state, 'I will do whatever you ask in my name, so that the Father may be glorified in the Son' (John 14:13). In order for us to receive whatever we ask, we have to ask for something God can lend His name to, something in accordance with His will and which He has already started to do.

To return to the point that we all need to have something to do, something to achieve, if life after this were to be simply lolling about on a cloud playing a harp for eternity, I wouldn't want it. (My granddaughter, who has just given birth to her first baby with all that that involves, remarked, 'It might be rather nice at weekends, though.') Fortunately, as we shall see, it isn't; it is far more exciting and fulfilling than that.

This double need which we all have – to be loved and to achieve – is simply the obverse of God's desire to love us and set us to work with Him in fulfilling His plan for the earth. He created us with those needs so that He may meet them. As St Augustine of Hippo put it, 'Our hearts are restless until they find their rest in you',[1] and Lady Julian of Norwich explained this truth from God's point of view:

> I am the Ground of thy beseeching: first it is My will that thou have it; and after, I make thee to will it; and after, I make thee to beseech it and thou beseechest it. How should it then be that thou shouldst not have thy beseeching.[2]

It is interesting that this double purpose revealed in the first book of the Bible, Genesis, is echoed by Paul in his letter to the

---

[1] *The Confessions of St Augustine*, Book 1, Chapter 1.
[2] Julian of Norwich, *Revelations of Divine Love* quoted in F. L. Houghton, *Amy Carmichael of Dohnavur* (The Dohnavur Fellowship, 1953).

Ephesians. The text I have already quoted about God choosing us before the creation of the world, is followed very shortly by:

For we are God's handiwork, created in Christ Jesus to do good works, which God prepared in advance for us to do.
Ephesians 2:10

So, yes, we were created simply because God wanted to do it; we were loved into being. But once we had arrived, God didn't wonder what He could do with us; He already had tasks for us to fulfil. The instruction to fill the earth and subdue it in Genesis chapter 1 is amplified in the next chapter:

The LORD God took the man and put him in the Garden of Eden to work it and take care of it.
Genesis 2:15

The next step was for God to develop man's capacity for love. He said, 'It is not good for the man to be alone. I will make a helper suitable for him' (Genesis 2:18). I have already referred to the human need to give love as well as receive it, which may be met to some extent in loving dolls and animals. However, although God had already created animals, the story continues:

But for Adam no suitable helper was found ... Then the LORD God made a woman ... and he brought her to the man.
Genesis 2:20, 22

The companionship of animals did not fully meet the need in man to love and be loved, so God created a helper, another human being complementary to the man. At this stage, before the perfect plan of God had been spoiled, there was no question of the woman being in any way inferior to the man. The word 'helper' does not imply that; the same Hebrew word *(ezer)* is used to describe God Himself when Moses says, 'My father's God was my helper' (Exodus 18:4), and he names his second son *Eliezer* – literally 'God and helper' – to commemorate that. No one would claim that because God was Moses' helper He was inferior to him.

So from the first two chapters of the Bible we have already discovered two reasons why we exist, what we are for. The first is to receive and give the love of God and of other human beings. This primary purpose is expressed in the summary of the law given by Christ Himself:

> 'Love the Lord your God with all your heart and with all your soul and with all your mind.' This is the first and greatest commandment. And the second is like it: 'Love your neighbour as yourself.'
> *Mathew 22:37-39*

With regard to God, our love for Him will, of course, be expressed to a large extent in worship. I once heard a famous actor deride the god he assumed that Christians believe in by saying that he couldn't accept a god who had such a view of himself as to demand that his creatures should worship him; he thought it insufferable pride on the part of such a god. In fact, as we have seen, our God invites us to share in His very essence – overwhelming, self-giving love. That is what lies at the heart of worship.

The second purpose in creating us is that we should join with God in fulfilling His perfect plan for the earth. Whatever his purpose may be for the rest of His creation is not our responsibility, but He has actually committed this earth and its welfare to us; we are to rule over it and He will act upon it only through us and with our cooperation. He has never rescinded that plan in spite of our devastating failure to fulfil it. We shall examine in the next chapter just what that failure was, but before that there is one more point I would make.

When the humans disobeyed God's command and ate the fruit of the tree of the knowledge of good and evil, the Bible states:

> Then the eyes of both of them were opened, and they realised that they were naked; so they sewed fig leaves together and made coverings for themselves.
> *Genesis 3:7*

It was only after they had sinned that they could appreciate what wrong was. Prior to that their life had been 'good', but they had not realised that was so because they knew no other state; they had nothing with which to compare it – they had not eaten of the fruit of the knowledge of good and evil. But when they had eaten, of course, they *did* know the difference between the two and, to their horror, they realised that they had been in a state of good (God had pronounced all of His creation 'very good' – Genesis 1:31), but now they were in a state of evil; they were sinners.

The story continues:

> Then the man and his wife heard the sound of the LORD God as he was walking in the garden in the cool of the day, and they hid from the LORD God among the trees of the garden.
> *Genesis 3:8*

Whatever Scripture means by 'the sound of the LORD God as He was walking in the garden' (and we will consider that in greater detail in chapter 3), it implies that this was something they were used to and they had previously had no need or desire to hide. They were in a perfect relationship with God and delighted in His company – as He did theirs. They did not have to be given a set of laws regarding how to live in that relationship, any more than there should be a need for a husband and wife to have laws instructing them how to

27

behave towards each other; if there is such a need, the marriage is already less than it should be.

I cannot leave this chapter without quoting the next verse in Genesis: 'But the LORD God called to the man, "Where are you?"' (Genesis 3:9). From the very first moment mankind disobeyed Him, God began to search for him and draw him back to Himself; such is His love for us. I wonder how many sermons have been preached down the years on those words of God to each one of us: 'Where are you?'

Chapter 2
The Law

There are two recognised types of law. The first is the legal system, relating to rules and regulations which are agreed or imposed by some authority such as a government. The rules or laws will vary from nation to nation, although some will almost certainly be common to all – e.g., it is forbidden to commit murder and theft. The Ten Commandments are an example of this type of law. Breaking these laws will incur some punishment or penalty, agreed and imposed by the authority.

The other type of law is the natural law, which is an intrinsic part of creation, such as the law of gravity. No authority or person has power to alter such a law. To break or fail to observe it does not carry a punishment or penalty but it will involve a consequence. To walk over the edge of a cliff will cause a person to suffer injury or death.

Most religions, including Christianity, believe there is a third form or source of law, similar to natural law, which is spiritual law There is an unseen spiritual dimension to life which exists alongside the material environment in which every human being lives and, for the Christian, this spiritual environment, unlike the material environment, is eternal. That is to say, it was, it is and it ever will be. What is more, it can be entered now. This is what Jesus was talking about when He began His ministry with the words, 'The time has come ... The kingdom of God has come near. Repent and believe in the good news' (Mark 1:15).

Some Christians, particularly those who have been brought up in the evangelical tradition, impose upon those words an understanding that Jesus must be referring to the fact that He has died for our sins and, if we confess those sins and accept Him as Lord and Saviour, then we are forgiven and cleansed and able to enter the kingdom of heaven.

Those facts are true, but Jesus made this proclamation at the very beginning of His ministry, before He had died and, in any case, there is no direct mention of sins. What confuses the issue is the word 'repent'. Many Christians have the idea that it means to confess their sins, and by the word 'sins' they are thinking of breaking the first type of law – the Ten Commandments, the legal laws of God. But 'repent' doesn't mean to confess your sins; literally it means to change your mind, to do an about turn. We have been going in one direction but now we stop and go in another.

Christianity holds that the natural person – that is, the person who is left to his or her own devices and is not guided by the Spirit of Christ – is going his or her own way rather than God's way. God has planned creation to work in a particular manner. There are the natural laws which everyone can recognise, and there are also unseen spiritual laws, and to break either will have unfortunate, indeed catastrophic, consequences. To repent means that a person who has been making him or herself the centre of life and going the way they choose realises that this is leading in the wrong direction. They turn round and begin going the way Christ leads them.

The problem with the world is that we are each of us out for ourselves. As we learn social skills we hide this to some extent, and we may even act generously towards others at some expense to ourselves, but when we get down to absolute basics, I am putting what I want ahead of what you want. I am making myself the centre of my world and trying to make you go round me; but, of course, you are making yourself the centre of your world and trying to make me go round you. We are all doing it, so it's no wonder the world is in such a mess.

The truth is, it isn't my world and it isn't your world; we didn't make it and we certainly didn't make ourselves. It is

God's world: He made it and He made us, and that means we have to recognise that He is the centre and we have been created to go round Him. Until we recognise that, we are part of the problem; when we recognise it and begin to live out in our lives the plan that God has for us, we become part of the solution. That is what it means to repent, and when we do that we become part of the kingdom of God, the kingdom of heaven; it is the same thing.

Of course, after we have been walking alongside Christ for a while, we will come to realise just how wrong the way we were going previously really was. The closer to Him we are, the more horrified we will be. It is then that we will be convicted – that is, when the reality of our sin will strike us. It isn't so much that we think we deserve a punishment or penalty, rather we realise that the way we had been going would lead to a dead end – literally a dead end; we would end up dead. That was its consequence because we were breaking or ignoring the spiritual law, just as walking over a cliff is breaking or ignoring a natural law. At that time we will feel the need to confess to Christ that we are sinners and beg Him to forgive us, and that is when we are ready to understand that all the evil that there is in the world, due to the ignorance and wilful selfishness of every one of us, was laid on Christ as He hung on the cross, and there it was dealt with once and for all. Somehow He absorbed it all; His goodness swallowed up all the world's evil, including our own, and we are set free to follow Him and work with Him to bring in the kingdom of heaven on earth.

When I became a Christian, I was taught that the good news was that Jesus had died for our sins, and if we confessed them and believed in Him we were given eternal life. That is gloriously true, but I do not think it is what Jesus meant by, 'Repent and believe the gospel' (although it will later lead to that). According to the proclamation quoted above, with which Jesus began His ministry, the good news was that the

Kingdom of God had come near and that all could enter it then and there if only they would repent – turn from their own way and walk with Him along his. Some Christians who understand at least the basics of the Christian faith may want to argue that a person cannot be saved until he or she has confessed that they are a sinner and claimed Christ's offer of salvation, but that isn't where Jesus began. He offered an alternative way of living – the way of God's kingdom.

Think of Peter, one of Christ's disciples. His brother, Andrew, has met up with Jesus and is obviously fascinated by Him and so he finds Peter and brings him to meet Jesus. Peter is captivated by Him also, and to such an extent that when Jesus invites him to leave his work as a fisherman and follow Him, he does so (John 1:40-42). Now that is a life-changing decision – it is repentance. At this stage, is Peter in or out of the kingdom? Even to ask that question indicates a legalistic view of what it is all about. Peter has responded to the invitation of Jesus, and I believe that Jesus would claim him as 'one of mine'. As Peter spends time with his new friend, watches how He treats other people and listens to His teaching, he must become aware that his own life isn't as attractive or fulfilling as it could and should be. What finally convicts him, however, is when Jesus enters the area of life which is Peter's forte – catching fish. Jesus tells His disciples to let down their nets, and the catch is so great that it is in danger of sinking the boat.

We are all different and will respond to different things because God deals with us on a personal basis. With Peter it was the fact that this wonderful man was a better master of his own trade than he was. That was when he saw himself fully for what he was – a sinner.

So often we put the cart before the horse and expect people to recognise that they are sinners before they have met Jesus. When I committed myself to Christ more than 60 years ago (I had been walking with Him reasonably steadily for many years before that), there was a moral standard more or less universally accepted by society. Most people were aware that they had failed to live up to it, so there was a sense of failure. Therefore, to preach the forgiveness of sins (even if that was not where Jesus began), met with some positive response. However, in our postmodern society there is no agreed standard of behaviour; each person does what is right in his or her own eyes. My idea of what is acceptable will be different from yours. Hopefully you will not seek to impose your views on me, and I must not seek to impose mine on you. So there is no plumb line by which behaviour can be universally judged and, therefore, no sense of sin – indeed, that word is no longer common currency. If, therefore, we believe that to preach the gospel means to tell people that their sins can be forgiven because Jesus died on the cross, we should not be surprised if fewer and fewer people respond. The great majority will not even begin to understand what we are talking about.

However, whilst there may be little or no sense of sin, many people are dissatisfied and feel that 'there must be more to life than this.' Perhaps Christ's approach is the one to try today. Of course, we won't use His actual words – 'The kingdom of God has come near. Repent and believe the good news' – but we might try to come alongside people (and that will take time) and sensitively tell them that we have a found a way of living our lives which is better than the way we had been living previously. We have changed direction (that's the repentance bit) and feel so much more fulfilled. If they seem interested, we can go on to explain about finding Jesus and walking with Him. That seems to me to be far more acceptable and worthwhile than trying to convince people that they are sinners (not the best way to win friends and influence people) so that, if we manage to succeed in doing that, we can then tell them that it is all right because their sins can be forgiven by Jesus who died on the cross.

I cannot stress too strongly that it is not our task to convict people of their sin – that is the work of the Holy Spirit. Our task is to introduce them to Jesus and allow Him to take them from there.

It is interesting that when Jesus first sent out the 12 disciples, He gave them the same words to proclaim:

> As you go, proclaim this message: 'The kingdom of heaven has come near.' Heal those who are ill, raise the dead, cleanse those who have leprosy, drive out demons.
> *Matthew 10:7-8*

There is no mention of sin, nor even the instruction to repent (although that is clearly implied) – simply the good news that the kingdom of God is near and the performance of signs to prove it.

The two trees

In order to explain what went wrong in God's plan for us to act as His stewards and rule over the earth, the Bible speaks of a garden with all sorts of trees bearing fruit which were good for food. At the very centre of the garden were two particular trees which are described as the tree of life and the tree of the knowledge of good and evil. God tells the man not to eat of the tree of the knowledge of good and evil because if he does, he will die.

Allow me to mention here that, contrary to what some Christians believe, it isn't important whether they were literal trees or symbolic. I believe that to insist on one or the other, and thus provoke an argument which may cause genuine believers to separate from each other, is a ploy of the devil who then gains a double advantage: it disrupts the unity in the Spirit which God desires (or, more accurately, commands) and, secondly, it diverts both parties from grasping the truth that God intends we should learn from the description of the trees. There obviously must be some symbolism here because I have never seen either the tree of life or the fruit of the tree of the knowledge of good and evil (there is no hint that it was an apple; where did that idea come from?). So what is it that God wants us to learn from the description of the two trees?

The fact that two trees are mentioned but God specifically commands that the humans are not to eat from one of them – the tree of the knowledge of good and evil – surely implies that they may, and indeed are intended to, eat from the other – the tree of life (see Genesis 2:16-17). It is here that many Christians misunderstand. They assume that because God said that if the humans eat of the tree of good and evil they will die, then if they do not eat of it they will live. But that is not so; if it were, there would be no need for the tree of life to be there because humankind would go on living for ever anyway, provided they did not eat of the one forbidden tree. But Scripture makes it crystal clear that that is not the case. When the humans do eat from the tree of the knowledge of good and evil, God says:

> The man has now become like one of us, knowing good and evil. He must not be allowed to reach out his hand and take also from the tree of life and eat, and live forever.
> *Genesis 3:22*

So the tree of life was not there to be an antidote to the consequence of eating from the tree of the knowledge of good and evil (i.e., death) in the way that a dock leaf is reputed to ease the pain of brushing against a stinging nettle. God specifically prevents the man from doing that. What is more, by saying that if, even in his disobedient and fallen state, the man were to eat of the tree of life he would live for ever, God is stating that, even in his innocent state, unless the man does eat of the tree of life he will *not* live for ever. The reality is that the man has been created and exists and then he is presented with a choice: eat from the tree of life and live for ever or eat from the tree of the knowledge of good and evil and die. Until and unless he eats of the tree of life, man is not immortal.

Some Christians claim that the human soul is immortal and will, therefore, exist throughout eternity either in heaven or in hell. The Bible does not support that idea. This is clear, not only from the verse quoted above from the Old Testament, but also in the New Testament: 'God, the blessed and only Ruler, the King of kings and Lord of lords, who alone is immortal' (1 Timothy 6:15-16).

According to Scripture, therefore, a person does not have immortality unless he or she is joined with God in some way, because only God is immortal. Human beings today are presented not with the choice of two trees but with Jesus Christ and the choice of following or rejecting Him:

Whoever believes in the Son has eternal life, but whoever rejects the Son will not see life, for God's wrath remains on him.
John 3:36

I must point out that 'eternal life' is much more than continuing to exist for ever and ever (I don't think I would want that); rather, it has to do with a new and enhanced quality of life, although it does include that new life being everlasting.

I have already said that I have never seen the fruit of the tree of the knowledge of good and evil; nor, of course, has anyone else. So what does it represent? I suggest that, placed as it is as an alternative to the tree of life, it represents the choice for mankind of being independent of God and making up our own minds of what is good for us and what is bad. Eating of the tree of life represents the willingness to surrender our desire to be independent and to trust that God, as the creator and designer of everything, knows what is best for us and what will yield the greatest joy and satisfaction (part of what eternal life involves), and so we choose to live in obedience and close relationship with Him. The problem for us is that we are not in the same situation as Adam in his innocence; we are descended from him in his disobedience and so we are not in a neutral state, able to choose which way we will go. We are born into a human race which is already living a life of independence from God and in which each decides for him or herself what is good and bad. Hence the need to repent, to decide to turn about and go with Christ. No wonder that was His opening message.

It is important to recognise that, so far in the story of creation, no laws of the legal type have been given to the human beings. Admittedly there is the command that they are not to eat of the tree of the knowledge of good and evil, but that is a warning rather than a law – similar to a notice reading, 'Do not approach the edge of the cliff which is subject to crumbling.' The possible *consequence* of ignoring that warning is death; it is not a legal penalty enforced by some authority. I suppose it could be argued that, since God is responsible for creating everything in such a way that to reject Him (symbolically described as eating of the tree of the knowledge of good and evil) leads to death, that is a built-in penalty; but to me that smacks of special pleading. It is much more reasonable to accept that, because God alone is immortal and He alone is the giver of life, to reject Him means that, separated from that only source of life, human beings must inevitably die; it is a consequence, not a penalty.

That leads us to a controversial issue amongst believers – the doctrine of penal substitution. As I share my own views on the matter (or, at least, as far as I have come at present in my understanding), I would stress again the need to preserve the unity of the Spirit. I share simply to provoke thought and

37

possible discussion, not to impose my views on anyone else. God is too big for anyone to grasp the whole truth about Him; let us, in humility, learn from each other's experience of Him.

Penal substitution

The doctrine of penal substitution claims that on the cross Jesus, who was Himself sinless, suffered the punishment for *our* sins. The illustration that I have used most frequently to explain it comes from the law courts of ancient times. A judge, an honourable man, found that his own son appeared before him on a charge of fraud. Of course, today their relationship would prevent such a thing happening, but not in those days. There was no doubt that his son was guilty, and the judge found him so, but then it came to the sentence. Everyone waited to see what it would be. When he announced it, there was a gasp from the assembled company; it was the largest fine permitted. But then, having passed sentence, the judge stepped down from the bench and paid the fine himself. That is penal substitution; bearing the punishment due to another.

There is another illustration I heard when I first became a Christian which I found far more difficult. It happened years ago at a summer camp for scouts. One of the lads had committed a very serious offence and had to be punished. The problem was that he was full of bravado, and the leaders were concerned that he should understand the seriousness of what he had done. They were undecided about how to get through to him. In the end, the scoutmaster called the whole troop together and explained what had happened, saying that the offence had to be punished and the sentence was 12 strokes of the birch (corporal punishment would, of course, not be permitted today). He then handed the birch to the assistant scoutmaster and said he would bear the punishment himself. Everyone else watched, including the scout who had committed the offence. Apparently it had the desired effect, because after the first few strokes the lad broke down, begging them to stop.

Now that is a very graphic illustration of what may seem a dry doctrine of penal substitution, but I found it deeply offensive. I was told that my revulsion was 'the offence of the cross', and that the cross *is* offensive and is supposed to be – it was a vivid picture of what it cost Christ to save us. I know that and I accept it, but I still found that particular illustration deeply offensive and I have never used it myself. I think my unease about it is to do with the fact that the punishment involved the deliberate infliction of pain. What good would it have done if it had in fact been exacted on the young culprit rather than the scoutmaster? The difficulty in discussing the case is that we do not know what the scout had done that was wrong. Justice – and there must be justice – requires that there should be some recompense. The first case imposed a fine following the crime of fraud, and this can be regarded as a form of recompense, but inflicting pain does not recompense anybody. When applied to Christ bearing our punishment on the cross, this can lead to the confused belief that the more pain Christ was caused, the more fully the justice of God was met. It gives a wrong picture of God, and over recent years I have become more and more concerned by this doctrine of penal substitution.

Let me set out the definition of the word 'penal'.

PENAL adj 1. of punishment: relating to, forming, or prescribing punishment, especially by law, the penal system
2. punishable by law: subject to punishment under the law
3. used as place of punishment: used as a place of imprisonment and punishment, a penal institution
4. payable as penalty: required to be paid as a penalty

(15th century. Via French pénal from, ultimately, Latin poenalis , from poena 'penalty'.)[3]

Notice that the total emphasis in that definition is to do with law and punishment. It is 'penal'; to pay the penalty for breaking the law. It smacks of reprisal, the desire to make someone suffer what they have made us suffer, and that is part of our fallen nature; it is not part of God. I may very well feel that I want to hurt someone for the hurt they have done to me but, even as I feel that, I know that it diminishes me. I just *know* that God isn't like that, and I want to be like Him; I don't want Him to be like me. In my better moments I don't want someone to suffer because they have made me suffer; that simply adds to the suffering there already is in the world. We must not assume that God thinks and acts as we do. '"For my thoughts are not your thoughts, neither are your ways my ways," declares the Lord' (Isaiah 55:8).

However, I am also very clear that people cannot be allowed to go on causing others to suffer and so, unless they stop doing that and begin to do all they can to alleviate suffering (i.e., they repent) then, in the eternal plan, they must be destroyed. It is here that the difference between the *punishment* imposed for breaking the legal law and the *consequence* of breaking the natural or spiritual law is highlighted.

This is such an important point that I want to develop it. Imagine a father and child walking along a pavement beside a busy road. He tells his child that he must not step into the road because he might get hurt or even killed. That would not be a punishment for stepping into the road; it would be a consequence. Now suppose that the child disobeys, lets go of his father's hand and runs into the road. The father sees a lorry

3 Microsoft® Encarta® Reference Library 2002. © 1993-2001 Microsoft Corporation. All rights reserved.

bearing down on the child so he rushes into the road and just manages to push the child to safety before the lorry hits *him* and injures him severely. Now that is not a punishment. The lorry driver did not say to himself, 'That father should not be in the road so I will punish him and cause as much injury as I can.' No one wanted to punish either father or child. Nevertheless, the father took the consequence of the child's disobedience; he took the place of the child and bore the *consequence* of his action.

Those of you reading this who are concerned that I am denying that Christ died in our place can relax. It was indeed a substitutionary death. It is the word 'penal' I object to. It wasn't God's *punishment* for our sin that Jesus was bearing; it was our sin itself and its consequence.

In Christ's parable of the prodigal son, the young man asks for his share of what would be his inheritance while his father is still alive and then spends it all on riotous living. It isn't simply the loss of the money; the desire of the son to reject his father and go off on his own must have been deeply hurtful, as well as the destruction of all his father's hopes for him. When the son returns, his father welcomes him back with joy; there is no question of punishment because the father himself bears the loss of the money and the hurt of the rejection.

We do not sufficiently appreciate what it cost God, our Father, to bear the consequence of our rejection of Him and of our sin. In some way, which we cannot fully understand, it involved the Godhead taking upon Himself all the wrong we have done to creation and to Him. When Jesus was on the cross, there was a moment when He cried out, 'My God, My God, why have you forsaken me?' (a quotation from Psalm 22). Some scholars argue that Jesus wasn't really forsaken by His Father; He only felt that He was. I do not agree. Sin cannot continue to exist in God's presence, and I believe that our sin laid on the Son tore God apart. As I have said, it wasn't God's punishment for our sin that Jesus was bearing; it was our sin itself. This is the truth Paul explains in his statement, 'God made him who had no sin to be sin for us' (2 Corinthians 5:21).

I am well aware that in the book of Isaiah we read, 'The punishment that brought us peace was on him' (Isaiah 53:5). So how can I claim that Christ bore our sin rather than our punishment for sin? Well, what was the punishment? We need to go back to the first act of disobedience – eating the forbidden fruit. God told the man, 'When you eat from it you will certainly die' (Genesis 2:17). It can certainly be argued that from the point of view of the man that was a punishment; indeed, under the law of our land we refer to legal execution as capital *punishment*. Those who regard this as punishment will claim that in suffering separation from His Father on the cross, Jesus was engaged in penal substitution. In that sense I can accept it. However, from the point of view of God, He wasn't imposing suffering along the lines of 'you disobeyed my command so it is only right that I make you suffer' – such suffering (as with the scoutmaster bearing the sentence imposed upon the delinquent scout) benefits no one. No, I believe it was a *consequence* of man's disobedience.

God's concern is not to make sinners suffer but to preserve the holiness of heaven. God's implacable opposition to sin – His wrath – must involve the destruction of all that is sinful, including man if he remains unrepentant. However, to believe that God says, 'I am going to make you suffer before I destroy you', dishonours Him.

Perhaps I ought also to refer to those verses where Christ's sacrifice is referred to as a propitiation or atonement for our sins (e.g., Romans 3:25; 1 John 2:2; 4:10). A propitiation is a theological term which refers to God finding a way to reconcile us to Himself while remaining true to His judgement on sin. Again, it is sin that He deals with; propitiation does not necessarily involve penal suffering.

If I have a dog which runs off and rolls in some foul-smelling bog, I cannot allow it into my home in that state. I am not seeking to punish the dog – I still love it dearly – but it cannot enter my home in that state. In the case of human beings, the question is what will cleanse us from our sin so that we may enter the kingdom of heaven? God's answer is, 'The sin has to be laid on the Lamb of God.' That is not a punishment; it is the remedy.

Let me return to the illustration of the father and his child. Because it is so important that the child does not step out into the road, his parents will probably introduce a *legal* law to prevent the child falling foul of the *natural* law. They will say, 'If you do what mummy and daddy have told you not to do then you will be punished.' Presumably these days they will not smack the child, but they might withhold a treat or send him to his room until he is sorry and promises not to do it again. It is important to understand that the punishment is a discipline for the child's good so that he will learn, under a *legal* law, not to break the *natural* law that if you are hit by a heavy-moving object you will be injured.

Once the child becomes an adult there is no longer need for the imposed legal law; he will know the danger for himself. In fact, the legal law is nowhere near as satisfactory as the child understanding for himself how to live. The legal law was only there to lead him to the truth, and any punishment is a temporary expedient to teach right behaviour; *it is not a reprisal*. Paul is making a similar point when he writes, 'So the law was our guardian until Christ came that we might be justified by faith' (Galatians 3:24).

Let us now apply that understanding to God's dealing with our failure to obey Him. Scripture says that God is too pure and holy even to look at sin. For a sinner to be near God is like putting a snowman next to a fire to keep warm – it will be destroyed. That is not a punishment; it is a consequence of a natural law. Similarly, for humankind to sin by disobeying God (breaking a relationship with God, a person, not breaking

His *law*) would result in death, not as a punishment but as a consequence of a spiritual law.

If God is the only source of life, then to separate ourselves from Him by choosing to be independent (eating from the tree of the knowledge of good and evil), and for that separation to be confirmed by God driving the humans from His presence out of the Garden of Eden, then the humans would rapidly lose not only contact with God but also any understanding of what He desires. Their descendants would have no memory or knowledge of a relationship with Him at all. So God gave them laws (The Ten Commandments) as guidance, but these were a very poor substitute for the personal relationship which God had planned (and which originally they enjoyed) whereby human beings would know Him and delight to please Him.

To go back to the illustration of the child, if he walks out into the road and is killed or injured, there is no point in seeking to punish him for disobeying the laws which were intended to keep him safe. So it is with Christ on the cross. He was not bearing our punishment for breaking legal laws – even if they are the laws of God. We are guilty of something far more serious: rejecting God Himself and His plans for us. That is our sin, and it is that which causes His wrath which will result not in our punishment but in our annihilation. By taking that sin – mine, yours and that of every other human being – upon Himself, Christ has experienced the full force of that wrath which, to use a phrase applied to storms, has blown itself out on Him.

Justice

Nothing that I have said regarding penal substitution implies that I do not believe in the need for justice. The complaint, 'It isn't fair', does not seem to be something we learn but, rather, to be something we are born with – part of what it means to be a human being. Selfishness may lead us to override it, but it is there.

To break a spiritual law has consequences. As I write this, the world is still suffering the aftermath of the almost global recession of 2008 that was caused by the greed of a number of reckless financiers. How much of the judgement on their actions was brought about by some direct intervention from God and how much by the working out of the consequence of breaking one or more of the spiritual laws which God built into them I do not know, but judgement it is.

To ignore the need for justice can lead to a misunderstanding of the command of God that we must forgive others who wrong us. The Lord's Prayer assumes that before we approach God we will already have done this – 'Forgive us our sins as we forgive those who sin against us.' (Incidentally, why is the wrong emphasis so often put on this wording in public worship? In most churches we hear 'as we forgive those who sin *against* us', whereas the whole point should be, 'Forgive us our sins as *we* forgive those who sin against *us*.')

A fundamental understanding of our God in both the Old and New Testaments is that He is just and that at the end of this life we will all appear before His judgment seat. For those of us who have accepted Christ as our Saviour, there will be no condemnation – not because we are innocent but because we have recognised our sin, confessed it and turned from it to walk with Christ. God forgives us not by overlooking our sin but because He laid it upon Christ on the cross. Jesus took our place by accepting the judgment of God on sin.

Sin must not be ignored; it has to be recognised and dealt with. The Christian faith does not proclaim that God forgives everyone; rather that forgiveness is available for all those who acknowledge their sin, turn from it and accept Jesus as their Lord and Saviour. That is why we should not rush in and command that someone must forgive everyone who has harmed them irrespective of whether those people have admitted their guilt. This is the secret of the success of Archbishop Tutu's 'Truth and Reconciliation Commission' in South Africa. What kept the nation from the conflict of reprisals was that the guilty under apartheid had to face their actions and confess their guilt before they could be reconciled to and by the state.

Having said that, however, just because someone who has hurt us has never admitted their guilt and apologised (and so we have not been able to offer them forgiveness), that does not give us the right or freedom to retaliate or even nurse a grievance. If we do that, we are harming ourselves; there is an area of our being which is bitter and twisted and, if it is harboured, it will damage our relationship with the Lord. God is unable to offer unrepentant sinners forgiveness and so they will have to face severe judgment, but He never ceases to love them and long for them to turn from their wickedness and live. So it must be with us.

Several years ago I was deeply hurt by the unkindness and selfishness of someone who never apologised. Had I tried to offer them forgiveness, I believe that would have caused resentment and would have made matters worse because they had no conception that they had done wrong and, had I pointed it out, they are likely to have claimed that they had a right to behave in the way they did. They have since died, but fortunately I was able to continue my relationship with them and treat them with kindness and respect and so, in that regard at least, I have a clear conscience.

So what about those who do evil and refuse to repent; what happens to them? The Bible states:

Do not take revenge, my dear friends, but leave room for God's wrath, for it is written: 'It is mine to avenge; I will repay,' says the Lord.
Romans 12:19

46

So God does promise justice. Is this a reference to hellfire? I will refer to the subject of hell in greater detail later, but let me say here that I find it difficult to believe that any suffering there may be will continue for ever and ever because, as we have already seen, the human soul is not immortal in itself, and Paul speaks of all rebellion being *destroyed*:

> Then the end will come, when he [Jesus the Son] hands over the kingdom to God the Father after he has destroyed all dominion, authority and power.
> *1 Corinthians 15:24*

So, is destruction to be the only consequence for those who have caused wilful suffering to others? That seems almost too merciful because they will simply cease to exist. I am not suggesting that they should be caused physical pain, even if they have inflicted this on others; that is simply retaliation and accomplishes nothing. So is there no alternative between annihilation and making them endure the same suffering they have caused? Perhaps there is. What if, before their destruction, they are shown the kingdom of God set up on earth as it is in heaven? That is to say, they see what they could have had, what they have missed. They will have to face the reality of what they have done and the way they have lived their lives. Although this idea is and can be only speculation, it is not entirely fanciful because Scripture states:

> For we will all stand before God's judgment seat. It is written: 'As surely as I live,' says the Lord, 'every knee will bow before me; every tongue will acknowledge God.' So then, each of us will give an account of himself to God.
> *Romans 14:10-12*

I also have in mind a strange verse relating to Christ immediately after His death:

He was put to death in the body but made alive in the Spirit. After being made alive, he went and made proclamation to the imprisoned spirits – to those who were disobedient long ago when God waited patiently in the days of Noah
1 Peter 3:18-20

These spirits are not the spirits of men. When that is what is meant, Scripture says so, as in 'the spirits of the righteous made perfect' (Hebrews 12:23). It seems that these spirits were fallen angels. And the words 'made proclamation' are not the ones used for 'evangelise' but mean rather to 'proclaim' or 'declare'. Maybe these spirits were hoping that finally Satan would prevail and they would be released from their prison. Christ went to tell them that He had triumphed through the cross and that Satan had been defeated and so they had no hope. Their punishment was to know that they had chosen the wrong leader and that all that awaited them was destruction. I imagine that to continue to exist until then but with that knowledge would be pretty hellish.

However, the Bible does not tell us much about what happens to those who refuse to accept God's offer of eternal life within His kingdom – only enough to know that justice will be done and right will prevail.

I close this chapter with the assertion underlying all that I have been seeking to explain. It was not God's original intention that human beings should be subject to laws (the legal sort) because we were designed to live in a relationship with Him, accepting that He knows what is best for us. The first man was given no laws, and we who seek to follow Christ as Lord and Saviour are similarly not under law; we are under grace. But that needs further explanation.

Chapter 3
The Bible (1)

From the Garden to the Exodus

On one occasion when I was acting as chaplain in a hospital and conducting a service of Holy Communion on one of the wards, a woman asked if she could be the last to receive the elements. I was happy to comply but I asked her why she wanted this. She explained, 'The Bible records that Jesus said, "Drink ye all of this", and so I would like to drink all of the wine that is left.'

I didn't point out that if all the others partaking in the service adopted her interpretation, a difficult situation would arise, nor did I spend time trying to explain that the words she quoted were a particular translation into English of what Jesus actually meant – 'Drink this, all of you.' I had the impression that her mind was made up and that nothing I might say would change it.

I still find her request rather humorous, but it illustrates the problems that may arise if we try to take every word of Scripture absolutely literally – even if the translation we use exactly reflects the meaning of the original, and that, in itself, is a major assumption. Some Christians adopt a test to assess how 'sound' (in their view) other believers may be by asking, 'Do you believe the Bible is infallible?' I find that question rather like the famous leading question in a court of law: 'Have you stopped beating your wife?' To say either 'Yes' or 'No' gives a misleading answer.

A belief in the verbal inerrancy of the Bible is comparatively recent. I suppose individual Christians may have held that view in earlier centuries as a personal belief, but it did not become a claim on a more general basis until the latter part of the nineteenth century. To ask if the Bible is infallible is the wrong question; wrong because the Bible is about God (who alone is infallible), and there are no words which can express all that God is. To answer, 'No, I don't believe it is infallible', implies that I think it is flawed, when I don't. I prefer to say that I believe the Bible to be the word of God – remembering that, as we have already seen, a word is a means of self-expression. So I believe that the Bible truly expresses what God wants us to know about Him, His plans for creation and our part in it. Bear in mind that the truths contained in the different books were written by different authors at different times and had to convey the truth to the people alive at the time they were written and all down the ages until now, and into the future.

Allow me to mention here something that can cause severe damage to the Christian faith. It has been summarised in the phrase 'God of the Gaps', and it refers to the approach of some believers to point to those things in creation which cannot be explained by science and claim, 'So there must be a God who did this or that.' The problem is that as scientific knowledge develops and *can* explain this or that, it destroys the *need* for the existence of God and this, in the eyes of some, destroys the very existence of God as well. As the gaps diminish, so does the God who supposedly fills them.

This problem is exacerbated by those who adopt the view that Scripture is literally true in every word it contains. But spiritual truths very often cannot be expressed in the literal meaning of words. Jesus Himself faced this difficulty in seeking to describe what the kingdom of heaven is. Time and again He said, 'The kingdom of heaven is like...' Of course, it isn't really a mustard seed or a treasure hidden in a field, but such illustrations widen our understanding and promote our imagination to accept the reality of something we have not yet experienced.

In the context of the description of the two trees in the Garden of Eden, God tells the man that if he eats of the tree of the knowledge of good and evil he will die. I truly believe that statement in the sense that the act would separate him from God who is the only source of eternal life. However, to claim that prior to that act of disobedience by man, no plant and no animal (including dinosaurs) had ever died *physically* is to draw more out of these verses than the Holy Spirit put into them. The Bible, and the opening of Genesis in particular, is not a scientific explanation of *how* God created everything. (In any case, that would have been far beyond the understanding of anyone alive at that time and, as I have said, Scripture had to make sense to them as well as to us.) Rather it is seeking to convey the truth of *why* God created everything and, in particular, the role of humankind within that creation. To hold to the view that God created everything over a period of six literal days of 24 hours may be an attempt to honour Scripture, but I do not believe it honours the Holy Spirit who inspired that Scripture. Indeed, I believe such an approach prevents those who hold it from appreciating the spiritual truth that the Spirit intended to convey. However, the error is far more serious than that because a scientist, or anyone else who accepts a theory of evolution, will be prevented, or at least seriously hindered, from becoming a Christian if they think they have to accept a doctrine of creation in six literal days.

Those who insist on holding to the literal truth of every word of Scripture sometimes give the impression that they believe their (and everyone else's) salvation depends upon it. It doesn't; we are saved by our faith in Christ and His work on the cross, not by believing in the infallibility of the Bible. The Church thought it was honouring God by excommunicating Galileo for claiming that the earth went round the sun, partly because the Bible speaks of the sun rising at one end of the heavens and making its circuit to the other (Psalm 19:6). We still speak of the sun rising and setting, but now we recognise the error of trying to defend something the Bible was not, in fact, claiming; we must not repeat that error.

I suggest that we should ask, 'What truth did the original authors wish to convey?' rather than, 'What is the literal meaning of the words they used?' Of course, that does not mean that the words are unimportant; we do need to know their meaning. I am simply stating what we all recognise – there are some experiences we have where words are inadequate.

There is another danger involved in our approach to the Bible: we may impose our own ideas on the words and totally misunderstand what it is saying. An illustration of this is the following text:

> If my people, who are called by my name, will humble themselves and pray and seek my face and turn from their wicked ways, then will I hear from heaven and will forgive their sin and heal their land.
> *2 Chronicles 7:14*

There are many Christians today who quote these words and assume that they can apply them to the land where they are living. Towards the end of the last century, Jimmy and Carol Owens of the USA wrote a thrilling Christian musical to be performed in churches all over the nation entitled 'If My People...' and used it to call upon God to honour that promise to heal their land. We in the UK imported it to be used for our land also. Much as I enjoyed the presentation, I have to admit that there was no justification for applying the text in that way. It was a particular promise given to Israel where the faith and the nation are combined in one. God had given them their own land. We Christians are called out of all the nations of the world and we do not have a land. Indeed, we are to live as 'aliens and strangers in the world' (1 Peter 2:11, NIV 1984). Peter tells his readers that they have an inheritance 'kept in heaven for you' (1 Peter 1:4); and the writer to the Hebrews spells it out even more clearly: 'Here we do not have an enduring city, but we are looking for the city that is to come' (Hebrews 13:14).

I do not doubt that the righteousness of believers within any nation will help leaven the lump of the whole, and of course, all Christians should pray for their land, whichever land that may be, but there is no justification for taking a promise which was given specifically to Israel and applying it to any or every nation where Christians are to be found.

The Bible is many things, and we have to come at its truth from a number of directions. To insist on taking every word, or even every phrase, totally literally may cause a person to miss the wood for the trees and to adopt a legalistic approach to the faith. What helped most in my own understanding of the Bible was when I came to see it as a record of real people setting down their experiences of encountering the living God. Because these experiences were genuine, this is what makes the Bible 'true' and reveals who God is. It is important to gather these experiences together and set them out as doctrines and creeds about the nature of God so that we can have a common basis of what we believe and determine what is truth and what is heresy. But, as we saw in chapter 1, we are not reasoned into faith, even if to have faith is not unreasonable. Personal testimony is still the strongest witness to the reality of God – 'this is how *I* have experienced Him.' It is this more than anything else that is likely to promote the comment, 'I wish I had your faith', even if the person making it is unwilling to do much about seeking it for themselves. It is for this reason, and in the hope that it will help others to seek the God I have come to know, that in the final pages of this book I will dare to set down some of my own encounters with Him.

In a very real sense, the Bible is a love story. It is the record of how, having created human beings in and for love and to care for His earth as His stewards, and having suffered the hurt of our rejection of Him and His plans, God pursues us to win us back to Himself. To attempt to comment on every major incident and theme in Scripture would make this book longer than the Bible itself and so I must be selective, but let us take up the story very near its beginning where humans are depicted as living in the beautiful Garden, in innocent and perfect relationship with God and delighting to carry out His task of caring for the earth and everything on it, and knowing that the fruit of the trees is good for food and they may eat of them all except the tree of the knowledge of good and evil.

A personal devil?

Scripture describes how the serpent tells Eve that it is unfair of God to prevent her and Adam from eating from the forbidden tree and says that He has done so only because He does not want them to become His equal, and, anyway, they won't die if they do eat of it. To get involved in an argument as to whether the serpent did actually speak using vocal chords is not only a pointless exercise (what does it really matter?), but I believe it is another ploy of the devil to distract us from recognising the truth that the author (inspired by God) wants us to understand – that the disobedience of the human beings was prompted by a source outside themselves, even if the suggestions fell on fertile ground.

Some Christians do not believe that there is a personal devil. When I was training for ordination, my vice principal held this view and he explained that the total absence of good is so terrible a state that this alone is sufficient to account for the evil in the world which is usually attributed to the devil. There is truth in that statement, but I believe it ignores the claims of the Bible.

Scripture clearly teaches that humans, together with the animal kingdom, are not the only created beings. There are angels, cherubim and seraphim, principalities and powers and several others. In speaking about children, Jesus remarked:

> See that you do not despise one of these little ones. For I tell you that their angels in heaven always see the face of my Father in heaven.
> *Matthew 18:10*

So there are angels in some sort of relationship with children; we speak of them colloquially as 'guardian angels'. Churches also have their angels – the letters at the beginning of the book of Revelation are addressed not to the churches but to their angels. I am not sure how you write to an angel, but it is such a strange instruction that it must mean something. Then, apparently, each nation has its angel or prince (Daniel 10:13), with God's own people, Israel, having an archangel – Michael (Daniel 12:1).

There is also a prince of the whole world who has become the Satan (adversary). This is not the place to enter upon a detailed analysis of angels and particularly of the devil. However, we must understand that the devil is not another god with the power of evil equalling the goodness of God. No, he must have been created by God because there is no other source of creation, and originally he must have been good because everything created by God must be good. We are given little information about what caused him to rebel against his creator, but there are strong hints that it was pride.

Jesus describes Satan as the prince of this world (John 12:31; 14:30; 16:11). Furthermore, when the devil was tempting Jesus he offered to give Him the whole world:

And he said to him, 'I will give you all their authority and splendour; it has been given to me, and I can give it to anyone I want to. If you worship me, it will all be yours.'
Luke 4:6-7

Some may argue that the devil is a liar and it was not true that the world was his to give to Jesus, but if that were so, Jesus had only to point it out – so it would have been no temptation at all. In fact, it was a very real temptation. Jesus had come to win the world, and here was the devil offering to give it to Him without the ordeal of the cross. How attractive that must have seemed, but it would have left God's creation in its fallen state and Jesus Himself a subject of the devil.

Finally, we must take into account the statement, 'We know that we are children of God, and that the whole world is under the control of the evil one' (1 John 5:19). This was written after the death, resurrection and ascension of Jesus, and it illustrates an important truth. We saw in the previous chapter that in spite of our sin, God has not changed His original plan to place humankind in charge of the earth as His steward and does not act on earth without our cooperation and prayer. Similarly, He has not yet removed the angel, who has now become the devil, whom He originally appointed as prince of the earth. Jesus defeated him but did not destroy him. That will happen, but not until Jesus returns with His saints to set up the kingdom of heaven on earth. Meanwhile, we have to contend with the devil in our lives and defeat him in the power of Christ.

Just a word of warning here: Satan may still be active and about his business of tempting humans to sin, but we do not have to succumb. Temptation can and must be resisted, even if it is difficult to do so. No one can claim, as one of my children did on one occasion, 'It wasn't my fault; the devil made me do it.' (It didn't work so he never tried it again.)

With mankind having failed Him, it is amazing to me that God didn't decide to abandon the whole plan, destroy everything that He had made and revert to existing only in the mutual love of Father, Son and Holy Spirit. He did, in fact, destroy almost everything, but not quite, when He sent a flood. Again, it is pointless to debate whether the waters covered the whole earth or only the whole of that part of it that was known to the writer of the story – remember that at that time everyone believed the earth was flat; it wasn't until about the third century BC that it was recognised as being round. Similarly, to insist that Noah took representatives of every animal, bird and insect into the ark strains the bounds of credibility. There are 24,000 species of butterfly and 140,000 species of moth (and I would be intrigued to know how Noah was able to differentiate between a male and a female caterpillar). To get bogged down in such detail is to miss the point of the story, which is that instead of abandoning the whole plan or destroying all that He had made and starting afresh, God preserves a remnant of creation in the ark. It is a sort of baptism of mankind – a going down into the water and coming out of it to be a new creation. God will not be thwarted; He relentlessly keeps to His original plan for mankind and the whole earth.

Abraham

As God commanded, human beings multiplied but, not being in a relationship with God, they followed their own devices. Once again, God works through a remnant as he selects Abraham and He plans, through him and his descendants, to create a people to be His own amongst all the other people on the earth.

It is here that we meet a very real problem. God demands that Abraham should offer his son as a human sacrifice. No wonder people recoil in horror and refuse to have anything to do with a God who could act like that. It does us, and God, no honour to deny that it is, indeed, a horrific demand. However, as I wrestled with the problem, I came to understand a truth which will explain many other difficulties in Scripture: *We must not try to impose our society and culture upon the society and culture pervading at the time of the stories we read in the Bible.* Remember that the people of Abraham's time did not know the true God. He had driven mankind from His presence because of their disobedience. Because He had made us to be loved by Him, there is a hole or space in our being, in our make-up, which was designed for Him to fill. Without Him, mankind is left with a sense of need for something or someone beyond ourselves and, not knowing the true God, we invent one of our own imagining. Different tribes and peoples will invent different gods, but it is interesting that universally these invented gods are demanding and need to be placated – what a travesty of the true God who longs that He should be known as a loving Father, even while we are in awe of His holiness.

Therefore, and this is the truth we need to remember as we read Scripture, God reveals Himself by degrees, step by step, as His people are able to receive that revelation. We who live this side of Christ's life, His death, resurrection, ascension and the outpouring of His Holy Spirit must not try to impute our far deeper understanding of God on to the people of the Old Testament. The Bible is a record of an ongoing and growing revelation of who God is and what He desires of us.

So, to return to the story of Abraham and Isaac; God said:

Take your son, your only son, whom you love – Isaac – and go to the region of Moriah. Sacrifice him there as a burnt offering on a mountain that I will show you.
Genesis 22:2

Notice the particular stress of the words, 'take your son'; that is bad enough, but then, 'your only son' and, so that there could be no doubt about the cost involved, 'whom you love', followed by the terrible demand to 'sacrifice him'. God had promised that Abraham would have countless descendants through Isaac, yet here He was demanding Isaac's death. The New Testament throws further light on Abraham's thinking:

> Even though God had said to him, 'It is through Isaac that your offspring will be reckoned.' Abraham reasoned that God could even raise the dead.
> *Hebrews 11:18-19*

At that time, many nations offered child sacrifices out of fear to placate their gods. Here was the true God asking Abraham to sacrifice his son, but out of love and obedience. The story might have been written by a gifted playwright in the way the agony is built up, because it contains the added horror that Isaac has to carry the wood on which he will die, followed by the lad asking his father, 'Where is the lamb for the burnt offering?' (Genesis 22:7). Can you imagine the father's agony? But the words of his reply – 'God himself will provide the lamb for the burnt offering, my son' (Genesis 22:8) – were more meaningful than he could appreciate. Yes, God did stay his hand as Abraham was about to slay Isaac and He did provide a ram which was caught in a thicket nearby, but many commentators on this passage point out that never again did God demand a human sacrifice from His people and, from the experience of Abraham, they learned that lesson.

Of course, we know another truth: many centuries later another Father took His son, His only begotten son, whom He loved, and offered Him as a sacrifice for the sin of the whole world. That son, also, had to carry the wood on which He was to die. For me, the parallel between the two stories is too vivid to be coincidence, especially as we know that the story of

59

Abraham was written down such a long time previously. The Bible is trustworthy and does indeed record faithfully those things God wants us to know.

Moses

God's 'remnant', the descendants of Abraham and Isaac, had increased to become several families, and the time came for the next stage of God's plan. A severe famine had caused this remnant to travel to Egypt where supplies of grain could be purchased, and eventually they settled there. Although, initially, they were honoured guests, with Joseph, Isaac's grandson, being appointed first minister to the Pharaoh, as time passed, a later Pharaoh made them the slaves of the Egyptian people and treated them harshly. It was this slavery which formed them into a people.

I am old enough to remember the Second World War. There was no time for party politics; government ministers were appointed on the basis of being the best man for the job irrespective of their previous party affiliations. The times and the tasks were too desperate for anything but total unity to face the common enemy. So it was with God's people under slavery – they had to bond together simply to survive under the harsh regime. What might have become warring tribes were forced to become one people. Nevertheless, the Hebrews, as they were known, continued to multiply to such an extent that the Pharaoh became alarmed that they might rise up in rebellion and overcome his own people. To reduce their numbers he ordered that all the Hebrew male babies should be killed at birth. One particular family placed their baby, Moses, in a basket in the reeds of the river near where the Pharaoh's daughter came to bathe. As they had hoped, she saw the baby and took him with her into the palace. Here he was brought up and educated. He had the opportunity to watch and assimilate the leadership skills that operated all around him – something he would never have experienced as an oppressed slave. The Hebrews themselves, in their intense suffering, would not have been able to recognise what God was doing. It is only later generations, standing back from the situation, who can see how God was creating a people for Himself and preparing Moses for his vital leadership role.

In their anguish, the Hebrews cried out to the God of their history but whom they hardly knew, and He had already prepared their deliverer. Moses, in spite of his upbringing in the Pharaoh's court, had learned of his birth as a Hebrew and mentally associated himself with his people. When, therefore, he saw a Hebrew being assaulted by an Egyptian, he killed the culprit, but had to flee for his life to the desert, where he became a shepherd (what a role shepherds play in God's plan of redemption). Here, although he retained the benefits of his education, he was removed from the influence of the Egyptian court and, in his hours of isolation, had time for thought and meditation.

The harsh oppression of His people and their cries for relief, combined with the preparation of Moses for his task, results in God taking action. He gains the attention of Moses by causing a bush to flame with fire yet not be consumed. (Once again it is important not to become sidetracked into debating how a bush could be in flames yet not destroyed. Scripture speaks of an angel appearing in the bush, so perhaps it was the blaze of his glory; but what does it matter how it happened? It had the intended effect.) It is such an unusual sight that Moses goes over to inspect it, and here he has an encounter with the living God who tells him that He has chosen him to be the deliverer of His chosen people. Immediately Moses makes excuses. It is interesting that many people called by God to a particular service try every trick of the trade to get out of it. Moses, in contrast to the response of the prophet Isaiah some centuries later (Isaiah 6:8), says, 'Lord here am I; send someone else' (Exodus 4:13, paraphrased).

One of the objections Moses makes is that if he were to go and tell the Hebrews that the God of their fathers had sent him to rescue them, they would say, 'Oh really? And what God might that be; what is His name?' (Exodus 3:13, paraphrased). They had become so far removed from God that they have no idea who He is or what He is like. Moses asks God how he should answer them.

Here we must pause, because this question is of immense significance.

Even in our own day, names have great importance. Every school teacher knows this. There is all the difference there can be between saying, 'You, the boy at the back with the red hair, stop talking,' and 'James Smith, that is the last warning you will get.' To know someone's name gives you some authority over them.

A person of influence, in a desire to help someone achieve something, may say, 'Mention my name to the person who interviews you.' Names can carry influence.

In the time of Moses, and, indeed, throughout most of the Bible, names had an even greater significance. It was believed that to know someone's name gave you power over them. I am told that there was one Pharaoh who was so determined not to surrender any power to any possible rival that he gave himself a special name which he would not divulge to anyone, not even his family. In that culture, therefore, for Moses to ask God to reveal His name is not only bold, it is almost blasphemy. It is both surprising and wonderful that God responds by revealing His name.

Here is the only true God, the creator, sharing Himself so deeply with His people that He allows them to have influence over Him. In addition, of course, it gives greater meaning to Christ's invitation for us to use His name in our intercessions to the Father.

A verb or a noun?

There is even more truth to be drawn from this encounter of Moses with His God: the name itself. In asking God His name, presumably Moses was expecting a proper noun as the answer, similar to Isis or Osiris – gods familiar to the Egyptians. Instead, God gives him a verb; the verb 'to be': I AM.

Many years ago a wise priest said to me, 'Try thinking of God as a verb rather than a noun.' I have found that immensely helpful. God is not static; He is active, constantly expressing Himself in recreating, upholding, redeeming, making new: God is energy.

In quoting God's reply, 'I AM', many Bibles have a footnote reading, 'Or, I WILL BE WHAT I WILL BE'. It is spiritually rewarding to meditate on both meanings for they yield much fruit. One truth is that whilst God does not change, our understanding of Him must, otherwise we will never grow in our faith. I have already explained that the revelation of God is a continuing process. He reveals Himself to His people step by step as they are able to accept that revelation, and we must not impose our understanding of Him on the people of the Old Testament and judge them for their limitations. Yes, God is the eternal I AM, but for His people on their journey towards Him, He will be what He will be.

Eventually, after much prevarication on the part of the Pharaoh who did not want to lose such a large source of unpaid labour, Moses led the people from Egypt to the borders of the Promised Land. Before they entered it, God gave them what to this day the Jews regard as a precious gift – His Law, the Ten Commandments. Moses himself had encountered God but, although God had shown them something of His power and His concern for them in sending various plagues on the Egyptians, the people had no idea of how they should think of God. Indeed, even while Moses was on a mountain receiving the Commandments, the people demanded that Aaron, the brother of Moses, should make an idol for them to worship in the form of a golden calf, so little did they understand about the God who had formed them to be His own. Unable to have any close relationship with God, not only did they not know what He was like, they also had no idea how He wanted them to behave, so He gave them basic laws – including one which expressly forbade the making or worship of idols.

As far as laws can go, the Ten Commandments are as effective as any and far better than most, but, as we have seen, even the most perfect laws are a poor substitute for a loving relationship. Furthermore, laws cannot cover every eventuality, and attempts to keep them lead to a proliferation of lesser, more detailed laws. William Barclay describes this process in relation to the prohibition of working on the Sabbath Day. If I pick up my child, is that work? No, say the legal experts. What if I pick up a stone? Yes, that is work. What if my child is holding a stone when I lift him …? You can see how it grows and what a burden it becomes. The Law was intended to bring freedom because you don't have to guess what God wants – He has told you and, rightly understood, Jews do see it like that. What is more, they – God's chosen people – are the ones to whom He has revealed it, so they are immensely privileged to have the Law.

The sacrificial system and the Tabernacle

As we have already seen, laws of the legal sort (as opposed to natural laws) have to be enforced if they are to be effective, and require some form of retribution for those who break them. The books Leviticus and Numbers set out detailed instructions as to what restitution is to be made when one person wrongs another, but they make clear that such wrongs are also a sin against the Lord because He desires that we love both Him and all that He has created. It is in these books that the sacrificial system is set out. Under this, the wrongdoer is to sacrifice a bird or an animal (exactly what it should be is laid down in some detail). In some cases, the penitent is actually to lay his hand upon the animal, identifying himself with it in recognition of the fact that it is taking what should be his place as the guilty party. In this way, the idea or principle of substitutionary sacrifice is introduced to the people of God, and it is closely linked to the overwhelming significance of the Tabernacle.

Page after page of the Bible is devoted to minute details of just how the Tabernacle is to be constructed, and it can appear fruitless and a waste of time to read them. Certainly we can become bogged down with the descriptions of height, length and width of the different materials to be used, but they are truly meaningful. Let me summarise something of that meaning when we stand back from the detail and see the whole.

Having left Egypt, the people were living in tents in the wilderness. There were so many of them that, to avoid chaos, order had to be imposed. Every time they pitched their tents they were to gather in specific areas depending on the particular tribe to which they belonged. Each tribe was always allocated the same area in relation to the other tribes. In the very centre of the camp was a courtyard bounded by a fence constructed of curtains hung from poles – so much easier to transport than panels of wood. In this courtyard was the Tabernacle, which was basically another tent, even if it was considerably larger than those of the families within their tribes.

The Tabernacle was God's tent, the place where He dwelt. What a vivid visual aid it was! Without complex theological explanations, even the simplest soul could understand that

Jahweh, their God, the I AM, was not some distant, uncaring, totally unknowable being; He was here, living with them. If their tents were in danger of being battered by some sudden storm, so was God's. God was in the very centre of their lives. Later, in the New Testament, Jesus is described as dwelling with us, and the actual word is 'Tabernacled' (e.g., John 1:14).

However, as the visual aid goes on to illustrate, there was no easy access for the people to approach God; the tent was surrounded by its fence. Here the importance of the detailed measurements is revealed. The fence was five cubits high; the average height of a man was four cubits, so no one could peer over the top. However, the Tabernacle itself was ten cubits high, so everyone from every tribe could see the top of God's tent. What a brilliant illustration to convey the truth that God was present with His people but, at the same time, no one could approach Him because He was holy and they were sinners.

There is more yet. There was one gap in the fence, at its far end. Anyone entering through this entrance could see the Tabernacle at the other end of the courtyard, but between them and the Lord's tent stood the altar where the sacrifices were burned. The Tabernacle itself was divided into two areas; the first was larger and here the priests could enter to minister to the Lord. Separated from it by a curtain was the Most Holy Place where the presence of God dwelt. Only the High Priest could enter here, and that on only one day of the year – the Day of Atonement, when he offered the blood of a bullock and the blood of a ram for the sins of the priests, including himself, and the sins of the people.

Once again, we have to marvel at the wonder of the Bible. Centuries before Jesus came to the earth to be the true Lamb of God by shedding His own blood for the sin of the world, Scripture describes in detail God's provision for the forgiveness of the sins of all humankind from the time of Adam to the time of Christ. The sacrificial system of the Old

Testament was an elaborate visual aid, temporally effective in itself, to prepare His people to understand the meaning of the true sacrifice to be made by Christ on the cross. The Tabernacle with its one entrance foreshadows the claim of Christ to be the only way for man to come to God.

> Jesus answered, 'I am the way and the truth and the life. No one comes to the Father except through me.'
> *John 14:6*

All this foreshadowed the role of Jesus to be the true High Priest who took His own blood, shed on the cross, into the presence of God in heaven. How can anyone claim that all this was just chance or coincidence?

When the people were no longer living in tents but were established in the land and dwelling in houses, the Temple was built in Jerusalem, modelled on the Tabernacle but double the size. When Christ died, the curtain separating the Holy Place in the Temple from the Most Holy Place was torn in two from top to bottom – again, a vivid visual aid proclaiming that the way into God's presence is now open to all who claim the sacrificial death of Jesus on the cross as their own.

So, with the people of God in the wilderness preparing to enter the Promised Land, let me recap on what God has accomplished so far in His plan to win humankind back to Himself. Having been compelled to drive human beings from His presence because of their sin, rather than destroy everything and everyone, He works through a tiny remnant, first with Noah and then choosing Abraham, to form a new people for Himself. From Abraham's son, Isaac, He brought forth Jacob who fathered the 12 sons from whom He formed the 12 tribes. Over the many years in Egypt, they multiplied and, being made slaves, they were pressured into becoming a close-knit people. He chose and prepared Moses to lead them out of Egypt towards the Promised Land. In the wilderness, because they did not know Him or His ways, He gave them the Ten Commandments as a guide to live by until such time as they were ready for a personal relationship to be restored. Yet, even then, He began to reveal Himself as the caring God who was so closely identified with them that He shared their life by having His own tent in their midst.

All was ready for the next stage of His plan of redemption.

Chapter 4
The Bible (2)

The Promised Land to the coming of Christ

When God first offered His people the opportunity to possess the Promised Land, they refused to enter because their reconnaissance team reported that, although the land was wonderfully fertile, it was already occupied by men who were so large that they felt like grasshoppers in comparison. In spite of the fact that God had delivered them from the powerful Egyptians and had miraculously provided water and food in the wilderness, His people still did not trust Him, so He had to discipline them until they were willing to obey Him.

When I was called up to do my National Service in the forces in 1946, the first six weeks involved hours of 'square bashing'. We marched up and down the parade ground until the 30 of us in the platoon acted as one at the command of our training sergeant. God did the same with His people in the wilderness, training them there for 40 years. He appeared before them as a cloud during the day and as a column of fire at night. When the cloud or fire moved, the people moved. In Scripture, a cloud often depicts the glory of God, and whilst it may seem unusual to us for God to manifest Himself in such a visible manner, remember that this is before the Holy Spirit was given to the Church. In those days, the Spirit was given only to a particular individual here and there whom God chose to fulfil a particular role, perhaps as a leader or a prophet. If all the people were to trust this person, there was a need for a clear manifestation of God's presence. When the cloud moved, the people would strike camp and set off to wherever it led them; when it stopped, they would erect their tents. Sometimes they might have just set up camp when the cloud moved again, and off they had to go; at others they might be in one place for several weeks or months. God disciplined them into obedience.

Finally, after the 40 years, God called His people to go in and take possession of the Promised Land of Canaan. It was already occupied by other tribes who, of course, were unwilling to surrender their territory and so the Israelites (as the Hebrews were to become known) had to fight for it, and this often involved fierce battles causing injury and death.

Once again, as with the offering of Isaac by Abraham, we are faced with a dilemma: is the God of the Old Testament different from the God of the New? Jesus – the clearest manifestation of God ever given to us – was described as the Prince of Peace. When He was arrested, He chose not to offer resistance or to fight; yet here we have the people of the Old Testament engaged in violent warfare at God's behest.

Let me say again that the Bible is a record of a continuing revelation of God and His ways. At this stage of the story every nation had its own god. Which was the best god to have? Well, obviously the god who most effectively looked after the people who worshipped him – the one who won the most battles. Our God has not and does not change; He is a God of peace, but it would have been utterly unrealistic to expect any nation, including His own people, to accept a god who did not enable them to win battles. Instead of deriding Christians for worshipping a violent God of war, sceptics should marvel at the humility and patience of a God who is willing to become, at least to some extent, the sort of God they were looking for in order to win their trust so that He could lead them on, step by step, as they were willing to accept the revelation, to understand the sort of God He really is.

In this connection we need to bear in mind the following instruction:

You must purge the evil from among you. The rest of the people will hear of this and be afraid, and never again will such an evil thing be done among you. Show no pity: life for life, eye for eye, tooth for tooth, hand for hand, foot for foot.

Deuteronomy 19:19-21

In its context, this refers to a wrong done by one person to another within the people of God (in particular, to someone bearing false witness) rather than to an enemy during warfare. But, as we shall see shortly, Jesus extended it to enemies in general. The final sentence, forbidding pity, seems to be unnecessarily cruel. However, two things must be recognised. First, if the unity of the people is to be preserved, all wrong perpetrated by one person against another must be stamped out immediately. Secondly, as we have seen in considering the place of law, justice must be done and be seen to be done. Nevertheless, we must recognise that in those days (and I regret to say in ours as well in some cases), if members of another tribe injured someone in yours, you would go over and beat up several of them to teach them not to do it again. In the light of this, to confine the retribution to one eye for one eye and one tooth for one tooth is a merciful limitation. The principle of forgiveness was a totally foreign concept (and still is in some cultures today). Many centuries were to pass before people would be sufficiently receptive for Jesus to be able to teach.

You have heard that it was said, 'Eye for eye, and tooth for tooth.' But I tell you, do not resist an evil person. If anyone strikes you on the right cheek, turn to them the other cheek also.

Matthew 5:38-39

As I have already explained, we must not impose on people living in the time of the Old Testament the far greater

71

understanding of God that we have following the revelation of Jesus. As we trace the history of God's dealings with the people of Israel, we need also to read the prophets who provide an insight into the purpose of what God was doing and where He was leading His people. Even while God was supporting them in battle, Isaiah was revealing something of His true nature.

He will judge between the nations and will settle disputes for many peoples. They will beat their swords into ploughshares and their spears into pruning hooks. Nation will not take up sword against nation, nor will they train for war anymore.
Isaiah 2:4

They will neither harm nor destroy on all my holy mountain, for the earth will be filled with the knowledge of the LORD as the waters cover the sea.
Isaiah 11:9

Here we have the secret of God's plan – to restore the original relationship He had with humankind before Adam's disobedience, and which is further revealed in the words of St John:

Now this is eternal life: that they may know you, the only true God, and Jesus Christ, whom you have sent.
John 17:3

To know God, and therefore what He wants, is far better than any law.

The desire for a king

The people of Israel were greatly blessed because God had chosen them above all other nations, and they alone had the privilege of having been given His Law. However, He had not chosen them because they were special; they were special because He had chosen them – something they constantly forgot. He had a purpose in choosing them: they were to be His witnesses. Having been given His Law, they were to keep it and, provided they did so, this would allow Him to bless them in countless ways. Not only would they win their battles but, having won them and settled in the land, their crops and their cattle would increase in abundance. Other nations, seeing their success, would say, 'These people are blessed by their God far more than we are by ours. Let's give up our gods, choose theirs and live like them.'

The problem about this was that God's people kept turning from His laws, and their lives were little different from those of the nations surrounding them (sadly, something that can be said of many of us Christians today), and so God could not bless them as He desired because that would be to condone their sin. It came to a head during the time of Samuel, who was one of their greatest and most godly leaders. Unfortunately, his sons did not follow in his footsteps, so:

> All the elders of Israel gathered together and came to Samuel at Ramah. They said to him, 'You are old, and your sons do not follow your ways; now appoint a king to lead us, such as all the other nations have.'
> 1 Samuel 8:4-5

Can you appreciate the grief this must have caused Samuel and, even more, God Himself? God had chosen Israel to be His witnesses to the other nations so that they would want to be like them, but here were His people wanting to be like the other nations, totally reversing His plan. So Samuel consults the Lord.

> And the LORD told him: 'Listen to all that the people are saying to you; it is not you they have rejected, but they have rejected me as their king. As they have done from the day I brought them up out of Egypt until this day, forsaking me and serving other gods, so they are doing to you. Now listen to them; but warn them solemnly and let them know what the king who will reign over them will claim as his rights.'
> *1 Sam 8:7-9*

Samuel duly spells out how a king would laud it over the people and exploit them, closing with these words:

> 'When that day comes, you will cry out for relief from the king you have chosen, but the LORD will not answer you in that day.' But the people refused to listen to Samuel. 'No!' they said. 'We want a king over us. Then we will be like all the other nations, with a king to lead us and to go out before us and fight our battles.'
> When Samuel heard all that the people said, he repeated it before the LORD. The LORD answered, 'Listen to them and give them a king.'
> *1 Samuel 8:18-22*

Once again we see the humility of our God. Although they had Him as their protector – far better than any human king – when His people refused to be content until they had a king like the other nations, He granted their request so that He would not lose total contact with them. He would patiently wait until they learned more about Him and would trust Him more fully. However, the Lord reserved the right to choose who the king should be and ordered Samuel to anoint Saul, although he soon proved unreliable and the Lord chose David to replace him.

David was to become the most successful king the people were to have (although he was far from perfect and on at least one occasion he used his power to his own advantage and God had to discipline him), and our Lord Jesus was later to be born as one of his descendants.

It was David who chose Jerusalem to be his capital city where the Temple was to be built. A recent television programme on the history of the area pointed out that although the Bible highlights the importance of both David and Jerusalem, in fact, other kings and cities that are hardly mentioned in Scripture had a far greater influence on the history of the Middle East, and the presenter claimed that the biblical record is seriously unbalanced.[4] But such criticism misunderstands the purpose of the Bible: it is not a history of the world, or even of the Middle East, any more than it is a scientific text book; it is a record of how God set about winning human beings back to Himself through the 'remnant' He had chosen. Other nations and their kings may be far more important in the eyes of secular historians, but they were not part of God's plan of salvation and so they receive little mention in the scriptural record. It is at the name of Jesus that every knee is to bow. In the final summation of all things, everyone in history will be judged on what they have contributed to the coming of the kingdom of God on earth – including we who have accepted the salvation won by Jesus Christ (see 1 Corinthians 3:10-15).

After the reigns of David and his son Solomon, there was a succession of kings. Some were godly but others certainly were not. But as well as kings, God provided prophets.

---

[4] *The Bible's Buried Secrets*, BBC2 (March 2011).

The role of the prophet

One of the great prophets of the Old Testament was Isaiah. Here he speaks of God's call to him:

> In the year that King Uzziah died, I saw the Lord, high and exalted seated on a throne; and the train of his robe filled the temple. Above him were seraphim, each with six wings: with two wings they covered their faces, with two they covered their feet, and with two they were flying. And they were calling to one another: 'Holy, holy, holy is the LORD Almighty; the whole earth is full of his glory.' At the sound of their voices the doorposts and thresholds shook and the temple was filled with smoke.
> *Isaiah 6:1-4*

Uzziah had been a reasonably godly king, but when he died the outlook was bleak; there seemed to be no godly person to succeed him. Isaiah was dismayed, and in his deep concern for the nation he sought the Lord in His Temple. Here he had an overwhelming experience of God's presence – greater than anything he had known before. He had a vision of the Lord seated on a throne in all of His glory and power. Isaiah got the message! Yes, God had yielded to the demands of the people and given them human kings, but He had never surrendered His own power and authority. He was the true king and His throne was high above anything on the earth. Unknown and unseen by the world, God was working out His purpose. Who should be on the earthly throne of Israel was important, but nothing like as important as who was ultimately in charge. No wonder Isaiah was able to assert with confidence, in the words we have already quoted: 'The earth will be filled with the knowledge of the LORD as the waters cover the sea' (Isaiah 11:9). That day will come!

Along with the vision, Isaiah heard God calling, 'Whom shall I send? And who will go for us?' (Note the Trinitarian 'us'.) And, unlike Moses, he responded, 'Here am I, send me!' (Isaiah 6:8).

Isaiah's call and subsequent career as a prophet began because he was concerned about a current situation. This fact explains the principal role of all the prophets – to interpret to the people what God was doing at any given time. As the Lord revealed that, very often He might reveal also how it would lead on to something He was planning to do in the future. But the prophet was not a fortune teller whose task was to predict the future; rather he was to explain to the people what their God was doing there and then in the situation in which they found themselves.

It was no easy job being a prophet. Jeremiah in particular found it tough. He was called by God to warn the people of coming judgment for their sins, which, as I have mentioned, is not necessarily the best way to win friends and influence people. He was so unpopular that he was threatened with death, and for a while he was imprisoned. He gives a deeply moving account of how he became so unpopular that he decided not to speak what the Lord had told him, but the warning was so urgent that, in spite of himself, he couldn't keep silent:

> Whenever I speak, I cry out proclaiming violence and destruction. So the word of the LORD has brought me insult and reproach all day long. But if I say, 'I will not mention his word or speak any more in his name,' his word is in my heart like a fire, a fire shut up in my bones. I am weary of holding it in; indeed, I cannot.
> *Jeremiah 20:8-9*

The warning was that, because of their sin, the people would be taken into exile by a foreign nation. As I have already mentioned, the Israelites were so proud of their status as God's chosen people who had been given the Land and the Law that they could not even imagine the possibility that He would send them into exile as the prophets were proclaiming. In their view, not only would that diminish *them* in the eyes of the other nations, but it would also diminish the Lord Himself, and they were convinced He would never permit that.

It was the prophet Amos who pinpointed Israel's sin – they did not care about the poor:

> You levy a straw tax on the poor and impose a tax on their grain. Therefore, though you have built stone mansions, you will not live in them; though you have planted lush vineyards, you will not drink their wine. For I know how many are your offences and how great your sins. There are those who oppress the innocent and take bribes and deprive the poor of justice in the courts.
> *Amos 5:11-12*

The people had been offering sacrifices, but only as a ritual; their hearts were not in it, and Amos said that God would not accept their sacrifices nor listen to their empty songs of praise. He spelt out what God really wants: 'But let justice roll on like a river, righteousness like a never-failing stream!' (Amos 5:24).

Hosea was a man with a tender heart. Like Amos, he also proclaimed God's judgment, but God also used his circumstances and personality to reveal His own feelings even as He punished His people. Notice the pain in God's heart:

> When Israel was a child, I loved him, and out of Egypt I called my son. But the more they were called, the more they went away from me ... It was I who taught Ephraim to walk, taking them by the arms; but they did not realise it was I who healed them. I led them with cords of human kindness, with ties of love. To them I was like one who lifts a little child to the cheek and I bent down to feed them.

Will they not return to Egypt and will not Assyria rule over them because they refuse to repent? A sword will flash in their cities; it will devour their false prophets and put an end to their plans.

Hosea 11:1-6

Hosea does more than report God's coming judgement; he reveals His true feelings:

How can I give you up, Ephraim? How can I hand you over, Israel? How can I treat you like Admah? How can I make you like Zeboyim? My heart is changed within me; all my compassion is aroused. I will not carry out my fierce anger, nor will I devastate Ephraim again. For I am God, and not a man – the Holy One among you.

Hosea 11:8-9

So, looking at the indifference of the rich towards the poor within their own nation, the prophets proclaimed God's punishment – exile in Babylon for His people for a period of 70 years. That is a complete lifetime. At the end of that period there will be few who will remember what it was like to live in the Promised Land. We have a snapshot of how the people felt during that time of exile, because it did indeed happen as the prophets had warned;

By the rivers of Babylon we sat and wept when we remembered Zion. There on the poplars we hung our harps, for there our captors asked us for songs, our tormentors demanded songs of joy; they said, 'Sing us one of the songs of Zion!' How can we sing the songs of the LORD while in a foreign land? If I forget you, Jerusalem, may my right hand forget its skill. May my tongue cling to the roof of my mouth if I do not remember you, if I do not consider Jerusalem my highest joy.

Psalm 137:1-6

The discipline of exile did its work – only when they had lost their land did the people truly value what they had had.

However, as the prophets stood in the counsel of the Lord, He revealed that after the 70 years He would bring His people back to the land He had promised would be theirs. They saw even further into the future, but it was more of a general impression than specific details:

They will live in the land I gave to my servant Jacob, the land where your ancestors lived. They and their children and their children's children will live there for ever, and David my servant will be their prince for ever. I will make a covenant of peace with them; it will be an everlasting covenant. I will establish them and increase their numbers, and I will put my sanctuary among them for ever. My dwelling place will be with them; I will be their God, and they will be my people. Then the nations will know that I the LORD make Israel holy, when my sanctuary is among them for ever.

Ezekiel 37:25-28

Of course, King David had died long ago, but he was a folk hero; the kingdom of Israel had never spread so far as it had under him and his son, Solomon. But in the culture of the people at that time there would be no problem in considering a descendant of David as representing David himself and, although Ezekiel could not have understood just how his prophecy would be fulfilled, Jesus was to be such a descendant.

In speaking of the return of the people at the conclusion of the 70 years of exile, there is an interesting statement by the prophet Isaiah. Babylon, where they were being held in captivity, was itself captured by the Persians and it was the King of Persia, Cyrus, who ordered the temple in Jerusalem to be rebuilt and for its treasures, which had been confiscated by the Babylonians, to be returned. He was also instrumental in organising the return of the Jewish people to their land. In predicting this Isaiah says:

> 'This is what the LORD says to his anointed, to Cyrus, whose right hand I take hold of to subdue nations before him ... For the sake of Jacob my servant, of Israel my chosen, I summon you by name and bestow on you a title of honour, though you do not acknowledge me. I am the LORD, and there is no other; apart from me there is no God. I will strengthen you, though you have not acknowledged me.
> *Isaiah 45:1, 4-5*

The word 'anointed' is the Old Testament equivalent of 'Messiah' – the title given to Christ, God's anointed one. Cyrus was a pagan – a reasonably honourable one, but a pagan nonetheless. Yet, unknowingly, he performed God's will. God is sovereign and eventually everyone and everything will acknowledge that.

Even as God was disciplining His people and gradually leading them on to become what He wanted them to be, there was a major problem that had to be dealt with – sin, and only God could deal with that. The disobedience of the first human beings not only affected the relationship between themselves and God, but it also affected all of creation, as we shall see. Ever since that first disobedience, no one has been born in an innocent state; we all have a bias to sin. The theological term for this fact is 'original sin'.

From our present standpoint we do not and cannot appreciate the horror and devastation of sin. The nearest we can come to it is to recognise what it cost God to put it right. I do not understand just how the death of Christ on the cross accomplished it, but the burden was so great and the weight of sin was such that it was manifested in the material realm and actually turned the world dark at midday (we know from the date of the Passover that there was no eclipse of the sun at that time).

Of all the prophets, it was Isaiah who was nearest to the truth as we who live this side of Christ's life, death and resurrection know it to be, but even he sees through a darkened window. It is as though he is peering through a mist and momentarily catches sight of a dim figure. He speaks of a servant of the Lord who obediently fulfils God's purpose. Sometimes it seems as though he is talking of the whole of the people of Israel acting as His servant; at others it is all focused on an individual. Sometimes he is talking of the future; at others it is as though that future is already in the past:

> See, my servant will act wisely; he will be raised and lifted up and highly exalted. Just as there were many who were appalled at him – his appearance was so disfigured beyond that of any human being and his form marred beyond human likeness.
> *Isaiah 52:13-14*

Yet, in spite of his tentativeness, his description of Christ on the cross (even though there is no mention of that dreadful instrument of torture) is so accurate that it can be only the inspiration of the Holy Spirit that enables him to predict just how God would deal with our sin:

> He was despised and rejected by mankind, a man of suffering, and familiar with pain. Like one from whom people hide their faces he was despised, and we held him in low esteem. Surely he took up our pain and bore our suffering, yet we considered him punished by God, stricken by him, and afflicted. But he was pierced for our transgressions, he was crushed for our iniquities; the punishment that brought us peace was upon him, and by his wounds we are healed. We all, like sheep, have gone

astray, each of us has turned to our own way; and the LORD has laid on him the iniquity of us all.
Isaiah 53:3-6

However, it was Jeremiah who, although he suffered so much because he faithfully proclaimed God's judgment, was finally able to reveal:

'This is the covenant I will make with the people of Israel after that time,' declares the LORD. 'I will put my law in their minds and write it on their hearts. I will be their God, and they will be my people.'
Jeremiah 31:33

I described the Bible as a love story – the history of how God set about winning mankind back to Himself, to restore that wonderful initial relationship between the creator and the creature when there was no need for laws to govern behaviour. We learn from the Old Testament prophets that, however things may appear to be, God is working His purpose out. They saw that the time would surely come when men and women would just know within themselves what our God desires, and it would be our delight to fulfil those desires and to dwell with Him:

No longer will they teach their neighbour, or say to one another, 'Know the LORD,' because they will all know me, from the least of them to the greatest,' declares the LORD. 'For I will forgive their wickedness and will remember their sins no more.'
Jeremiah 31:34

Addendum: between the Old and New Testaments

There are some 400 years between the return of the Jews from exile and the birth of Christ. The protestant Bible contains no writings which deal with this period. Much of the history which affected the Jews is recorded in the Apocrypha, which is recognised as being part of the Bible by the Churches of Rome and many in the East.

Following the invasion by the Babylonians, Israel did not regain its sovereignty until after the Second World War. Palestine was occupied by one nation after another as power changed hands. It was during this period that Alexander the Great dominated so much of the area and attempted to Hellenise the nations he conquered, including the Jews. This led to the production of the Septuagint – a translation of the Old Testament into Greek – which was used by the Jews who no longer lived in the Promised Land.

In time, the Greeks gave way to the Romans who developed means of communication within their empire, in particular by building roads. With the Scriptures available in an international language and travel being made easier, the way was being prepared for Christianity to spread throughout the world.

During the exile in Babylon, the Jews obviously could not worship at the Temple and so, unless they were to be absorbed into the faith of the pagans around them, they were compelled to find an alternative. It was at this time that they set up local synagogues, with attention being given to the reading and exposition of the Torah (the Jewish Bible – the Law in particular). Also, because it was no longer possible to offer the prescribed sacrifices, they concentrated more on personal piety and prayer.

Although it may seem that little happened over these 400 years or so, in fact, God was continuing to lead His people on and preparing for the next stage of His plan and purpose.

Chapter 5
Jesus

In thinking about Jesus we in the West have a problem – He comes with a halo – that is to say, the first fact we are told about Him, or the one that first registers with us, is that He is God. We may differ in our understanding of just what 'God' means, but all of us will have the impression from the outset that Jesus is not really like us. For the people surrounding Him at the time, the problem was the opposite – He was exactly like them; He was just another man:

> Coming to his home town, he began teaching the people in their synagogue, and they were amazed. 'Where did this man get this wisdom and these miraculous powers?' they asked. 'Isn't this the carpenter's son? Isn't his mother's name Mary, and aren't his brothers James, Joseph, Simon and Judas? Aren't all his sisters with us? Where then did this man get all these things?'
> *Matthew 13:54-56*

The truth is that Jesus was both God and man. If the problem for those who lived alongside Him was to believe He was God, for us it is to believe He was man. I have learned from experience that when I seek to explain what I am about to share, those who listen or read seriously misunderstand what I say or write, so let me state clearly from the outset that I believe that Jesus was, is and always will be God. That is who He eternally is in His essential being and so, whatever else He may be, He can never cease to be God. Whether or not you agree with my understanding of some other things about Jesus, please hold firmly in mind that I am convinced that when He became man and during the whole of His earthly ministry, Jesus never ceased to be God.

Down the ages, countless books have been written about Jesus, and here am I devoting just one chapter to the subject (although, of course, He is central to every other chapter also). I will, therefore, have to be highly selective, with the aim of encouraging further thought and discussion about particular aspects of His life, teaching and actions.

Instead of starting at the beginning, I will start at the end – at the very last evening that Jesus spent with His disciples. Scholars differ in their views of whether or not at that time the disciples believed He was God. There are grounds for holding that it was only after His resurrection and ascension that they came to realise that He was the Son of God as well as the Son of Man. (The latter, incidentally, seems to have been His preferred description of Himself.) There is no doubt, however, that they realised that He had a very special relationship with God, to whom He referred as 'Father'. Admittedly, Peter had recognised that Jesus was the Christ, the expected anointed one of God, although that did not imply that He was actually God incarnate. Nevertheless, they all understood that He was a gifted teacher, healer and miracle worker.

As I say, it is the final evening Jesus is to spend on earth with His disciples. The Last Supper is over and Judas has already left to betray Jesus to the High Priest. Jesus knows that time is short and that He is about to be taken from them, and so He seeks to reassure them:

Do not let your hearts be troubled. You believe in God; believe also in me. My Father's house has many rooms; if that were not so, would I have told you that I am going there to prepare a place for you? And if I go and prepare a place for you, I will come back and take you to be with me that you also may be where I am. You know the way to the place where I am going.

John 14:1-4

It is Thomas who complains that they don't know where Jesus is going and so they can't know the way. Jesus replies that He Himself is the way to the Father, and if they really knew Him they would know the Father as well; in fact, they do know the Father and have seen Him. This prompts Philip to ask, 'Lord show us the Father' (verse 8).

This request devastates Jesus – read the whole passage to pick up the shock that He experiences. He knows that Judas is on his way with a guard from the High Priest to arrest Him, and here is Philip revealing that he and the others have a total misunderstanding of what He has been doing over the past three years and how He has been doing it, but there is no time to set their thinking straight.

> Jesus answered: 'Don't you know me, Philip, even after I have been among you such a long time? Anyone who has seen me has seen the Father. How can you say, 'Show us the Father'? Don't you believe that I am in the Father, and that the Father is in me? The words I say to you I do not speak on my own authority. Rather, it is the Father, living in me, who is doing his work.'
> *John 14:9-10*

Philip's request that Jesus should show them the Father reveals that all along he and the other disciples have been thinking that Jesus has the power within Himself to work the miracles they have witnessed. 'No', says Jesus, 'You have been watching the Father doing His work through me.'

This truth, recorded by John, is preserved also by Luke in the Acts of the Apostles, in his description of Peter explaining to the crowd the work of the Holy Spirit:

> Fellow Israelites, listen to this: Jesus of Nazareth was a man accredited by God to you by miracles, wonders and signs,

which God did among you through him, as you yourselves know.

Acts 2:22

If Jesus performed His miracles in His own power, then there was a wonderful three years or so while He was on the earth, but He was about to return to the Father and so the teaching and the miracles would all cease. However, God's plan was that the earthly ministry of Jesus should be only the beginning. The disciples, and those who responded to them and their teaching, were to carry it on so that the good news would spread across the world and down the ages. And what is the good news? Why, the statement He made at the outset of His ministry – that the kingdom of heaven had been brought near and could be entered now. The whole of the teaching of Jesus was to develop and amplify that, to explain what it meant, and the miracles were a demonstration of its truth: the kingdom was present now.

Why Jesus was baptised

When Jesus became man, Scripture says that He became an empty vessel (remember, He never ceased to be God):

Who, being in very nature God, did not consider equality with God something to be used to his own advantage; rather, he made himself nothing by taking the very nature of a servant, being made in human likeness.
Philippians 2:6-7

The word translated as 'nothing' literally means 'emptied'. It is also used in Paul's first letter to the Corinthians where he says that God had sent him to preach the gospel, 'not with wisdom and eloquence, lest the cross of Christ be *emptied of its power*' (1 Corinthians 1:17, italics added). So I take this to mean that Jesus gave up the authority and power which He had in heaven and became like us; or, rather, He became like Adam – man as He was in his innocent state, without sin. I believe that in His earthly ministry Jesus had no power in Himself which is now denied to us. Of course, being without sin meant that His *relationship* with the Father was not damaged. That in itself was a tremendous advantage, but *He had no power to work miracles.* I believe that He was in a similar situation to the disciples after His resurrection. They had been cleansed from their sin (Jesus, of course, was always without sin) and they believed that Jesus had risen from the dead, but He told them to remain in Jerusalem until they had 'been clothed with power from on high' (Luke 24:49). He expanded on this, saying, 'You will receive power when the Holy Spirit comes on you' (Acts 1:8).

I suggest that, being fully identified with us as man, Jesus, also, received power when the Holy Spirit came upon Him in the form of a dove at His baptism. New believers often ask the question, 'If Jesus was sinless, why did He need to be baptised?' Some commentators say that it was because He wanted to be fully identified with us in our humanity. I don't agree; I believe that because He already *was* fully identified with us (powerless in our own strength), he needed to be baptised with or in the Holy Spirit in order to receive power for His ministry. He had not given up His deity but He had emptied Himself of His divine power.

> Jesus gave them this answer: 'Very truly I tell you, the Son can do nothing by himself; he can do only what he sees his Father doing, because whatever the Father does the Son also does.'
> *John 5:19*

Jesus perfectly aligns Himself with His Father's will so that the Father may work His works through Him. John constantly makes this point in recording the words of Christ – see John 5:30; 8:28; 12:49 and also 10:37-38.

When I was very young I was given a book which, I think, was entitled *The Child Jesus*. In it there was a story about Jesus as a young boy finding a bird with a broken wing. He cupped His hands around it and when He opened them the bird flew away fully healed. Oh dear, oh dear; how I wish people would not try to gild the lily. The story is total heresy because, apart from the fact that the event never happened, it repeats the error revealed on the part of the disciples which so horrified Jesus on that last evening – it implies that Jesus, even as a child, had power to work miracles. Scripture states specifically that the first miracle that Jesus performed was to turn the water into wine at Cana in Galilee (John 2:11), and that was *after* He had been baptised with the Holy Spirit.

The writer to the Hebrews comes at the same truth from a different angle; he explains:

Therefore, when Christ came into the world, he said: 'Sacrifice and offering you did not desire, but a body you prepared for me; with burnt offerings and sin offerings you were not pleased. Then I said, "Here I am – it is written about me in the scroll – I have come to do your will, my God."'
Hebrews 10:5-7

Jesus did not die only on the cross; there is a sense in which He died at every moment of His life to His own desires and presented the body which His Father had given Him as an empty vessel to be filled with the Holy Spirit so that the Father might work His work through Him.

Let's be quite clear: when Jesus was lying in the manger He was not saying to Himself, 'You all think I am just another baby, but I know I am God!' He was fully human, with a human body and a human brain. He had to learn the things we all learn – how to walk, how to talk and so on. As He grew up, He would have heard about the expected servant of the Lord of whom Isaiah had spoken. Because there was no barrier of sin, He would have enjoyed a particularly close relationship with the Father and would have been devoted to serving Him, but He had no reason to think this was anything unusual.

You will recall that when He was 12 His parents mistakenly left Him behind in Jerusalem. Incidentally, that is not as careless as it may sound. It was at the age of about 12 that Jewish boys assumed a new status of becoming responsible under the law. (This is continued today with the ceremony of bar mitzvah.) On the journey from Galilee to Jerusalem Jesus would have been regarded as a child and would have travelled during the day with the women and other children. On the way back, with His new status, He would have travelled with the men but, of course, Joseph would not have been used to having Jesus with him on such a journey. It seems that it was only in the evening when Mary and Joseph met up that they discovered that each had assumed Jesus was with the other. They rushed back to Jerusalem and it took them three days to discover that He was with the learned teachers in the Temple. (Can you imagine their distress and panic over that time?) Like all parents, in their relief they blamed Jesus for not staying with one or other of them. However, it is the reply that Jesus gave that is so interesting: 'Well, where did you think I would be? Surely you realise I have to be concentrating on my work for my Father?' (see Luke 2:49). It is almost as though He adds – 'Isn't that so with everyone?' Only gradually would it have dawned on Jesus that other people didn't seem to be as single minded as He in seeking to discover all He could about God.

As time went on, it must have passed through His mind that perhaps He was to be the expected Servant/Messiah. Surely Mary would have told Him of the strange events at His birth when first the shepherds and then the wise men visited Him, followed by the prophecy of Simeon about Him (Luke 2:25ff.). I can imagine Jesus trying to thrust such thoughts out of His head as being big-headed.

Forgive me for sharing a personal reflection. I remember when I began to wonder whether God was calling me to ordination, I rejected the thought (partly because I didn't want it – more of that later) because I felt totally unworthy. When the thought became persistent and could no longer be ignored, in some trepidation I began to make enquiries and I let the family know what I was doing. The casual remark of one of them, 'I am not surprised; I don't know what took him so long to do it,' was a tremendous relief – apparently it wasn't just me being deluded. If I felt like that over becoming just one of countless priests, I can only dimly imagine how Jesus must have felt in wondering if He was to be the unique Messiah, and who was there in authority who would confirm that He was right?

When Jesus was baptised and the Holy Spirit came on Him in the form of a dove, John explains:

> And I myself did not know him, but the one who sent me to baptise with water told me, 'The man on whom you see the Spirit come down and remain is the one who will baptise with the Holy Spirit.'
> *John 1:33*

The fact that specific reference is made to the Holy Spirit remaining on Jesus implies that prior to that He had not remained; that is to say, when Jesus became man He was not already filled with the Holy Spirit. (Incidentally, John the Baptist was! The angel told John's father, Zechariah, 'He will be filled with the Holy Spirit even before he is born' (Luke 1:15).) The baptism of Jesus was accompanied by a voice from heaven, and here there is an interesting divergence between the Gospel writers. Matthew records the voice as saying, 'This is my Son, whom I love; with him I am well pleased' (Matthew 3:17). However, Mark and Luke record the words as, 'You are my Son, whom I love; with you I am well pleased' (Mark 1:11 and Luke 3:22).

This throws light on the working of the Holy Spirit:

The Spirit searches all things, even the deep things of God. For who knows a person's thoughts except their own spirit within them? In the same way no one knows the thoughts of God except the Spirit of God.
1 Corinthians 2:10-11

The Holy Spirit does not translate the Father's words; indeed, within the Trinity there is presumably no necessity to use words at all (what language would they use – Aramaic, Latin, Greek?). Rather He *interprets* the thoughts of God. I do not believe there is any discrepancy here. The crowd at the baptism needed to hear God's thoughts as 'This is my Son', whereas Jesus needed to hear, 'You *are* my Son. You are not getting above yourself; what you are doing is in accordance with my will and delights me.'

Before looking at what happened immediately after Christ's baptism, let me jump ahead briefly to that first miracle of turning the water into wine. How do you think Jesus would have felt? After all, He had never performed a miracle before – what if it didn't work? Presumably He had been strongly prompted by the Holy Spirit to do this, and on that first occasion it would have been simply an obedient act of faith. So it is with us as we first commit ourselves to belief in God – suppose He isn't there after all?

Faith is an interesting subject to consider. A veteran paratrooper jumps from the plane with complete confidence; a novice is scared stiff but jumps nevertheless. Which of them shows the greater faith? I suggest that whatever the state of their confidence, from a practical point of view their faith is equal: each relies equally on the fact that his parachute will open.

Forming a strategy

Directly after His baptism, Jesus goes into the wilderness. Scripture says that He was sent there by the Holy Spirit for the purpose of being tempted by the devil (Mark 1:12) – so even in that situation God was in command rather than the devil. I suggest that the purpose was for Jesus to experience from the outset what He was up against and to confirm His understanding of His role as the Messiah and His willingness to embrace it. He fasted for 40 days and it seems that it was during this time that He sought God's guidance as to what He was to do and how He should do it. Remember that, following humankind's disobedience in the garden, God began the task of winning man back to Himself to fulfil His original two-fold plan of having someone else to love and to serve Him in taking dominion over the earth as His steward.

Jesus saw His task as bringing fallen creation within the kingdom of God. Everything He did was centred on the kingdom. He began His ministry with the words, 'The kingdom of God has come near' (Mark 1:15); His principle teaching in the Sermon on the Mount was all about the sort of people who will be found in the kingdom and how they will behave; and the kingdom was on His heart in the days after His resurrection, before He returned to His Father: 'He appeared to them over a period of forty days and spoke about the kingdom of God' (Acts 1:3).

Almost certainly, over those days in the wilderness Jesus was working out the strategy for His ministry. We have already considered the devil's offer to give Jesus all the kingdoms of the world if only He would worship him, Satan;

but what of the other two temptations? After fasting for 40 days it must have been a real temptation for Jesus to turn stones into bread – but how would that forward the kingdom? That would have been a purely selfish act to meet His personal need at the time. What about the temptation to throw Himself off the pinnacle of the temple and have angels catch Him and lower Him gently to the ground? That would have been eye-catching and would have gathered a crowd, creating a sensational start to His ministry; but would it have had any bearing on changing the minds of people? No, it would simply create a desire for more and more wonderful signs – indeed the miracle of feeding the 5,000 did just that. When Jesus challenged them with the demands of following Him, the whole 5,000 drifted away and only the little band of disciples was left (John 6:66-67). No, the call to repent – to change your mind and the direction of your life – is the only way for people to enter the kingdom of God.

People come into the kingdom one by one as they see the truth and decide to live by it. But there was only one Jesus; how could he, alone, contact everyone? I believe that in the wilderness, in communion with His Father and guided by the Holy Spirit within Him, He decided what His strategy should be. He would share not only His message but also Himself, first with a small group who would watch what He did and listen to what He taught. When they had begun to grasp what the kingdom was all about, they would share it with others, and they with others in turn. In this way, eventually it would spread throughout the world.

It seems that Jesus was convinced that the Father wanted Him to begin by confining Himself to working with His own people, the Jews. On one occasion, this caused Him to act in a manner which seems completely out of character. He had been ministering almost without ceasing and was desperately in need of a break.

Leaving that place, Jesus withdrew to the region of Tyre and Sidon. A Canaanite woman from that vicinity came to him, crying out, 'Lord, Son of David, have mercy on me! My daughter is demon-possessed and suffering terribly.' Jesus did not answer a word. So his disciples came to him and urged him, 'Send her away, for she keeps crying out after us.' He answered, 'I was sent only to the lost sheep of Israel.' The woman came and knelt before him. 'Lord, help me!' she said. He replied, 'It is not right to take the children's bread and toss it to the dogs.' 'Yes it is, Lord,' she said. 'Even the dogs eat the crumbs that fall from their masters' table.' Then Jesus said to her, 'Woman, you have great faith! Your request is granted.' And her daughter was healed at that moment.

Matthew 15:21-28

Many commentators seem to think that this event depicts Jesus in a poor light and, presumably in order to save what they see as His reputation, they suggest that Jesus only temporarily rejected the woman in order to encourage her to persist and thus increase her faith. But why should we not take the situation and Christ's words at face value and allow Him to look after His own reputation? She did not belong to His own people, the Jews, and if He acceded to her request, in her joy she would obviously tell everyone she met what had happened, and anyone who needed healing or had a sick relative would besiege Him. He had to resist the temptation to spread Himself too thinly and become diverted from His mission. She had presented Him with a real problem, and He meant what He said when He explained that He had come to minister only to His own people, the Jews. Her brilliant and heartfelt reply about the crumbs under the table convinced Him that the Father wanted Him to honour her faith, and He granted her request. Even so, He immediately left the area and returned to Galilee.

This event was echoed later, but this time Jesus responded differently:

> Now there were some Greeks among those who went up to worship at the festival. They came to Philip, who was from Bethsaida in Galilee, with a request. 'Sir,' they said, 'we would like to see Jesus.' Philip went to tell Andrew; Andrew and Philip in turn told Jesus. Jesus replied, 'The hour has come for the Son of Man to be glorified.'
> *John 12:20-23*

Here there was no request for a miracle; these were Gentiles who were interested in talking with Jesus, presumably about His teaching. Although He had confined His ministry to the Jews, the kingdom is for everyone irrespective of race or their current creed. Limiting His ministry was simply the strategy to achieve His purpose of reaching the whole world through those who had grasped the truth and would share it with others. The fact that these Greeks had come to Him, rather than having to wait until there were sufficient believers to go to them, convinced Jesus that the world was ready to receive the good news. The time had come for Him to depart and leave the task in the hands of His disciples and all who would believe in Him through their word and witness. The hour had come!

The future and the Holy Spirit

So, let us to return to that last evening when Jesus realised that Philip and the others had misunderstood how He had preached so effectively and performed the miracles. The shock and dismay because of the short time available before He would be arrested was replaced by the certainty that the Holy Spirit would continue His ministry through the disciples:

But the Advocate, the Holy Spirit, whom the Father will send in my name, will teach you all things and will remind you of everything I have said to you.
John 14:26

When they had been filled with the Spirit, the disciples would reflect on all that Jesus had done and taught and would see things in a different and true light. Jesus was free to depart without anxiety about the present lack of understanding on the part of the disciples. As He continued His final explanations, He said:

I have much more to say to you, more than you can now bear. But when he, the Spirit of truth, comes, he will guide you into all the truth. He will not speak on his own; he will speak only what he hears, and he will tell you what is yet to come. He will glorify me because it is from me that he will receive what he will make known to you. All that belongs to the Father is mine. That is why I said the Spirit will receive from me what he will make known to you.
John 16:12-15

Many great teachers of the faith emphasise the fact that Jesus is the greatest revelation of God ever given to humankind, and we will be given no greater revelation in the future until we see Him face to face. I believe that is true, but I would enter two caveats in the light of the passage quoted above.

There is further truth to be discovered within that revelation. Jesus declared, 'I have much more to say to you, more than you can now bear.' That confirms my belief that God's revelation of Himself is a continuous process according to the ability of human beings to receive it. We have seen that He could not tell the warrior tribes of the Old Testament to love their enemies, only to restrict their retaliation to one eye for one eye and one tooth for one tooth. Personally, I believe the Holy Spirit still has further truths to reveal as He searches the deep things of God (1 Corinthians 2:10). Let me quote the words of John Robinson way back in 1620 when the Pilgrim Fathers set off in the 'Mayflower' for America. They were members of his congregation and so this is a pastor speaking.

I charge you before God ... that you follow me no further than you have seen me follow the Lord Jesus Christ. If God reveals anything to you by any other instrument of His, be as ready to receive it as you were to receive any truth by my ministry, for I am verily persuaded that the Lord hath more truth to break forth out of His Holy Word.[5]

What a humble man he was, but isn't that great? I hope you have that view of Scripture. There is still more truth to break forth from it. We are God's people and we are still on the journey. This is a living Word and our God is a living God who 'will be what He will be'.

At the time the New Testament was written, slavery was a fundamental basis of the economic structure of many cultures. A literal reading of Scripture might encourage us to believe that God is in favour of it. Paul tells slaves to obey their masters. No doubt that was an argument put forward against Wilberforce and the others who worked for the abolition of slavery. At the time of the New Testament, God could not get through to people the truth that slavery is wrong; they were not ready for it. It took 1,800 years for the truths of the gospel to work in the understanding of believers for them to realise that the brotherhood of men – in particular the brotherhood of all believers – means that no one should be a slave to anyone else. I find it difficult to believe that only 200 years ago sincere Christians were happy to accept slavery, and some actually engaged in the slave trade. However, it is very likely that

---

[5] *The Congregational Magazine, 1845, New Series, Volume. XI.*, p504

Christians in the future will be disappointed that we tolerate today practices which will be abhorrent to them as the Holy Spirit continues His work of leading God's people into all the truth.

My second reservation is to explain that even Jesus, as God incarnate, was unable to reveal the totality of just who God is. It is true that all the fullness of God dwelt in Jesus (Colossians 1:19), but no human body can express that total fullness. Imagine a flautist attempting to play Beethoven's fifth symphony on his instrument. The opening bars are so famous that, even played on the flute, most people would immediately recognise them and, if asked, would confidently say, 'It is Beethoven's fifth symphony.' Well, it is and it isn't; even Beethoven himself could not express the fullness of his symphony on a single flute. Yes, Jesus expressed all that God is as fully as it is possible for a human body to do, but there is so much more to God than such a body can reveal.

The last week

John's Gospel has 21 chapters; ten of them (almost half) deal with the last week of Christ's life. His Gospel was written after the other three, when he had had a lifetime to contemplate the significance of all that Jesus had taught and done, and in telling the story he believed that the last week was crucial. Although the other three do not devote as great a proportion of their record to it, all that they write leads up to Christ's death and resurrection. To see Jesus simply as a great teacher is to miss the whole point. Yes, His teaching was all about the kingdom of God and how to live it, but without the cross and the empty tomb, none of us can have a place in the kingdom anyway.

There is so much to say about the cross and all that it means that I will not attempt to cover the doctrines that seek to explain it. I have already explained why I, personally, reject the doctrine of penal substitution and believe it was not God's punishment of sin that Jesus bore, but sin itself. I will confine myself to making two simple but profound comments.

First: we have made such a mess of living in the present world due to our pride, selfishness and wilful rebellion against God – that is, our sin – that I can accept without question that none of us can be admitted to the kingdom of heaven, if it is to remain the kingdom of heaven, unless that sin is dealt with; that is, the nature within us which has led to us committing sins in the past and which will inevitably lead to us committing sins in the future. Even with all that I have read and contemplated about the cross, I still do not fully understand just how Christ's death did deal with it, but I accept with the deepest gratitude the truth that indeed it did.

My second comment springs from that, and is very practical. Whatever anyone else thinks of me, and some may like me and some may not, I am very conscious of the fact that I am not the person I would like to be, let alone the person God created me to be. There have been occasions (perhaps fewer than there should have been) when I have been desperately ashamed of what I have done; so ashamed that I haven't known what to do with myself. The fact – and it is a fact even if I cannot understand it – is that God laid my sin on Jesus (yes, I know, how could He lay on Jesus a sin I had not yet committed? but God lives in eternity), and when I have confessed it, I am free of condemnation, first by God and as a consequence also by me. This is the most glorious truth and freedom I have experienced: I really am forgiven. Furthermore, in some way, that old sinful me died with Christ. Unfortunately, although it is dead it won't always lie down. However, there *is* a new nature within me; I have not yet become the person I was created to be but I am making progress.

This leads on to Christ's resurrection. The cross and the resurrection are inextricably linked. Without Christ's death sin has not been dealt with; without His resurrection death still holds sway and so there was no benefit in His sacrifice. Those who have lost someone they love will know just how devastating death is. But when Christ rose from the dead on that first Easter morning, a fundamental change was accomplished in both time and eternity. Death has been defeated – not yet destroyed, but defeated – because death could not hold Christ; He rose from death. His resurrection is the victory and guarantee that He will raise us also. Until then, no one could be certain that death was not the end; maybe people who died went out like the flame of a candle. The Sadducees, who held the Jewish faith, did not believe in a resurrection, and although others, like the Pharisees, did believe it, no one could be sure about it because no one had ever done it. Jesus was the first to rise from the dead.

Without a resurrection there is no real purpose in life. If this were the case, it would probably be better to live a decent life, considerate of others, but it really doesn't matter much in the long run; nothing is of any ultimate value. Why not grab all you can in this life? It is the only one you will have.

The resurrection changed everything. What you do and the person you become in this life are of eternal value because they survive into the future. Because of the work of Christ, there *is* a future – an eternal future. The fact of the resurrection is so wonderful that it has to be celebrated, in particular on its anniversary each year – Easter Day – but every Sunday is a miniature Easter Day. This is why the period of Lent has 46 days rather than just the 40 that commemorate Christ's days of temptation in the wilderness. It may be Lent, but we must continue to celebrate the resurrection every Sunday.

The resurrection appearances

The accounts of the resurrection in the four Gospels of Matthew, Mark, Luke and John do not entirely agree. There are minor differences of detail: just when did the women go to the tomb? How many of them were there? Mark says there were three women and that it was just after sunrise; John refers only to Mary Magdalene who went there while it was still dark. These apparent discrepancies don't worry me. For me, they make the whole thing even more authentic because I believe that the Gospel writers were setting down eyewitness accounts of different people who were saying, 'This is *my* experience of the risen Jesus – this is what happened to *me*.'

That truth is expressed in the wording of the 1662 Communion Service. I am not a traditionalist; I welcome the modern liturgies, but I was brought up on the old Prayer Book, and I love the words of administration set out there – 'The body of our Lord Jesus Christ given for *thee*,' 'the blood shed for *thee*.'[6] It is right that we remind ourselves in our modern liturgies that there is only one bread and that we are one body and are in fellowship with each other, but our unity is founded upon the fact that we each have a personal relationship with the same Lord Jesus Christ. And I suggest that we see something of that in the record of the witnesses to the resurrection.

Initially, the indication of the resurrection was not the appearance of Jesus but the *dis*appearance of His body. Mary found the tomb empty and assumed that someone had taken the body away. The Gospels say there was an angel (some say two) who told the women, 'He has risen! He is not here.' Then they add this; 'But go, tell his disciples and Peter, "He is going ahead of you into Galilee. There you will see him, just as he

---

6 *Book of Common Prayer* (1662).

103

told you"' (Mark 16:6-7). So the original plan was that the women and disciples should believe the fact of the resurrection simply on the word of the angel. There was no intention that anyone should actually *see* Jesus on Easter Day. He would not appear to them in Jerusalem; they would have to wait until they returned to Galilee to see the resurrected Jesus. But Mark adds an interesting detail. He records that the angel said, 'But go, tell his disciples and Peter, "He is going ahead of you into Galilee"' (Mark 16:7). Why the words 'and Peter'? Peter *was* one of the disciples.

Although we cannot be certain of the reason, I suggest that Peter must have been beside himself with grief and shame. All the disciples had run away, but Peter had denied even knowing Jesus, and he had done it not once but three times! And now Jesus was dead. Peter could never tell Him he was sorry. What is more, all the other disciples knew that Peter had denied his Lord. What is more yet, he had actually boasted in their presence that even if everyone else deserted the Lord, he wouldn't do so. And when Jesus warned him that before the cock crew the next morning Peter would have denied Him three times, Peter had insisted, 'Even if I have to die with you, I will never disown you' (Mark 14:31).

It is a wonder to me that Peter didn't commit suicide. I am sure he was in an agony of conscience and didn't know how to live with himself. It is as though, in heaven, the angel is told, 'When you give the message to the disciples that Jesus is alive, make particularly sure that *Peter* knows.' They all needed to know it, but Peter especially. Our Lord is a personal Lord and understands what each of us needs.

It seems, therefore, that there was a change of plan. The faith of both the disciples and the women was weaker than the Lord had hoped. The disciples didn't believe the report of the women, and very probably the women didn't even themselves believe the angel's message. Mary, in particular, was utterly disconsolate. It is as though our Lord could not bear to see her suffer so much. If her faith was not sufficient for her to believe the word of the angel (and, goodness knows, to receive any message from an angel takes some believing in itself), then the Lord, in His compassion, would meet her need; He would appear to her immediately, personally, and not wait for Galilee.

It is when He speaks her name, 'Mary', that she recognises Him (John 20:16). Spontaneously she goes to clasp Him in her joy. But the Lord has to teach her that things are not the same as they had been. She is not to cling to His physical presence any longer; and even as He gives her the joy of realising that He is alive, He has gently to rebuke her, to prepare her for the change in relationship. He *has* a body, the same body, but it has been transformed into a resurrection body. But the relationship is still there – He calls her by name. Jesus meets Mary's need and deals with her personally.

Then there were two more disciples – not members of the inner group of 12, but probably they were amongst the 72. They may well have been husband and wife. Luke just says that 'two of them were going to a village called Emmaus' and records that one of them was a male named Cleopas. Emmaus is some six miles or so from Jerusalem. Luke records their conversation, and we sense their depression. 'We had hoped that he was the one who was going to redeem Israel.' That says it all, doesn't it? 'We *had* hoped.' It is as though the heart of Jesus compels Him to reveal Himself to them also. Before they left Jerusalem they had heard the report because they explain:

Some of our women amazed us. They went to the tomb early this morning but didn't find his body. They came and told us that they had seen a vision of angels, who said he was alive.
Luke 24:22-23

But their faith also is weak – they don't believe it. Their need is different from Mary's. Hers was a matter of personal relationship with Jesus; theirs is more rational. They were looking for the Messiah, the one who would deliver Israel. So for them, as Luke explains, beginning with Moses and all the prophets, Jesus goes through the Scriptures to show how the Messiah must suffer. They do not recognise Him until He breaks the bread over the meal they have invited Him to share – presumably because then they see the nail marks in His hands – and at once He vanishes (Luke 24:13-31).

So they rush all the way back to Jerusalem to give the good news to the others. But when they get there, before they can say a word, the others tell them, 'It is true! The Lord has risen and [and listen to this] has appeared to Simon' (Luke 24:34). The special message from the angel that Peter, above all, should be told that Jesus was alive and would meet them in Galilee wasn't enough. Like the rest, Peter hadn't the faith to believe on the word of the angel via the women, so the Lord appeared to him personally. We are told nothing of what happened between them – only that Jesus came personally to Peter to meet his need. Later, in Galilee, Peter would be restored and recommissioned, the Lord asking him three times if he really did love Him – one for each denial. So the two who had rushed back from Emmaus (and remember they would have had to do that in the dark) had to listen first to the news from the ten (we learn later that Thomas was not present with them at this time) and those with them; only then are they able to tell of *their* meeting with Jesus on the road.

They are still talking about this – the appearance of Jesus to Peter and to the two from Emmaus – when Jesus appears to them all. They think He is a ghost. Their reaction is exactly the opposite of Mary's: she thought He still had the same physical body He had had before, so He had to tell her not to cling to Him. *They* thought they were looking at a ghost. so He showed them the wounds in His hands, feet and side and deliberately ate some food in front of them to prove that He was real. Jesus varied His appearances so that they met exactly the needs of those who saw Him.

As noted above, Thomas wasn't there on that occasion, and when the other disciples told him, 'We have seen the Lord!' he said to them, 'Unless I see the nail marks in his hands and put my finger where the nails were, and put my hand into his side, I will not believe.' A week later Jesus appears to the disciples again, and this time Thomas *is* with them, and Jesus says to him, 'Put your finger here; see my hands. Reach out your hand and put it into my side. Stop doubting and believe' (John 20:24-27).

I disagree with commentators who assume that Thomas did just that. I don't believe it; I mean, would you want to handle the actual wounds? And anyway, that is to miss the point. When the other disciples were telling Thomas that they had seen the Lord, Jesus was not there; they were *reporting* the fact, and he didn't believe them. Thomas was telling the other disciples – and only them – that he needed the proof of examining the wounds for himself, even to putting his fingers in the nail marks in His hands and his hand into the spear wound in His side.

When Jesus does appear to Thomas and the others, the Lord offers the very proof Thomas has demanded *and uses the identical words*. Jesus is revealing that, although no one saw Him at the time, He was aware of every word Thomas had uttered. I believe it was that that broke Thomas and brought the confession, 'My Lord and my God!' (John 20:28). He didn't *need* to handle the wounds, and certainly John does not record in his gospel that he did so. Far more wonderful than that is the vivid revelation of the truth which Jesus was to share with His disciples immediately before He returned to heaven, 'And surely I am with you always, to the very end of the age' (Matthew 28:20).

These witnesses to the resurrection all had a personal experience of Jesus which exactly met their need. It is true that Jesus died for the whole world (John 3:16) and that He died for the Church (Ephesians 5:25), but He died also for each of us as individuals – 'the Son of God, who loved me and gave himself for me' (Galatians 2:20). Perhaps we need to remind ourselves more frequently than we do that we are part of the body of Christ and that He adds all who are being saved to the community of the Church (Acts 2:47), but it is all based on a personal relationship with each one.

In view of that, perhaps I should sound a note of warning. Because Jesus deals with us all individually, we must not impose the way He meets with us on everyone else. Some like formal services with choirs singing anthems and with colourful vestments, ritual and incense. Others prefer informality, choruses, guitars and ministers wearing their everyday clothes. Enjoy what is right for you but don't despise what is right for others. God is bigger than we can imagine.

Before leaving the matter of the resurrection appearances, I would like to point out an interesting fact. In many of the cases, perhaps the majority, Jesus was not immediately recognised. Mary mistook Him for a gardener. One commentator suggests that this might be because the text states that she had been looking into the tomb when she turned to find Jesus standing there, possibly with the sun behind Him, and her eyes had not adjusted to the light and she could not make out His features. This smacks to me of special pleading, especially when we consider that the two on the road to Emmaus – who, remember, spent a considerable time walking alongside Him – did not recognise Him; in fact, the record states that they were kept from doing so (Luke 24:16). Then there is the appearance of Jesus at the lakeside in Galilee, speaking from the shore and directing the fishing disciples where to cast their nets. Again, some would explain this by saying that they were too far away to recognise Him, but the record says that they were less than 100 metres out, and Peter was able to get out of the boat and wade ashore (John 21:4-8).

So what might all this imply about Christ's resurrection body? First, it carried a very close relationship to His earthly body because 1) it bore the wounds of the nails and spear thrust from the crucifixion and 2) no body was left in the tomb; it was the same body but transformed. On the other hand, it was not subject to the physical restrictions of a human earthly body; it could appear anywhere and was not hindered by walls and barred doors, yet it could be touched and could cope with food (Luke 24:37-43). We should be careful here because the situation was temporary. The resurrection body which we are to have will be for use in the context of the promised new heaven and new earth, whereas the resurrected body that Jesus presented to the disciples was in the context of this earth on which we are living now in our untransformed bodies.

The ascension

This is important both for what happened and for what it means. Over the 40 days following His resurrection, Jesus appeared and disappeared on a number of occasions. Suppose this had simply stopped; almost certainly, doubts would have arisen in the minds of believers. Had something gone wrong and Jesus had been prevented from getting back to them? No, it was important that the disciples should witness His departure, His return to His Father. The problem about the way it happened is that it can endorse the false belief that God is 'up there'. I suppose it is important to think of heaven as being 'up' from this earth, but only in a similar sense to that of a child going 'up' from junior to senior school. Jesus was not propelled into space. As is so often in Scripture, the cloud that took Jesus from the sight of His disciples was a manifestation of the glory of God. He was returning to His heavenly Father, not going to another place in the planetary system.

This means that Jesus has taken His resurrection body into heaven. Prior to His incarnation, Jesus had no human body; nor, of course, did the Father or the Holy Spirit. A human body, transformed into a resurrection body, has been taken into heaven and become a forerunner, a guarantee that we also shall receive a resurrection body in the future. That is what happened, but what does it mean?

It means that we have an advocate in heaven. It isn't that the Father has no compassion or concern for us – we have only to consider all that I have detailed so far of how He has been at work to draw us back to Himself – but the Father has never experienced the restriction of being confined to a human body, nor has He experienced temptation, and certainly not the horror of sin, whereas Jesus experienced the full force of temptation (everyone else has given way to temptation in some area of their lives before that temptation reached its zenith) and, although He Himself did not yield and He remained sinless all His life, He experienced the effect and horror of sin when the sin of the whole world was laid on Him on the cross. With obvious reference to the High Priest ministering in the Tabernacle and the Temple under the Old Covenant, the writer to the Hebrews explains:

> For we do not have a high priest who is unable to feel sympathy for our weaknesses, but we have one who has been tempted in every way, just as we are – yet he did not sin.
> *Hebrews 4:15*

Although Jesus did not give way to temptation, that does not make Him despise us who have and who do. Rather, it enables Him to understand our weakness. The writer continues:

> Therefore he is able to save completely those who come to God through him, because he always lives to intercede for them. Such a high priest meets our need – one who is holy, blameless, pure, set apart from sinners, exalted above the heavens. Unlike the other high priests, he does not need to offer sacrifices day after day, first for his own sins, and then for the sins of the people. He sacrificed for their sins once for all when he offered himself.
> *Hebrews 7:25-27*

The death, resurrection and ascension of Christ effected and guarantee eternity for all who submit to Him as their Saviour and Lord.

Chapter 6
What happens now?

So here we are. We have been born and we have not yet died. We have responded to Christ's call, 'Repent and believe the good news' – that is to say, we have turned from going the way that our old nature was taking us and now we are determined to go with Christ on the path He is leading us. As I have said already, we have been given a new nature (something Jesus described as being 'born again'), but although the old nature has been defeated, it keeps rearing its ugly head and leading us off in the wrong direction again.

Fortunately, Christ does not reject us but is willing to accept us on the basis of what we truly desire to be rather than what we actually are. Theologians summarise this truth by the term 'justification by faith'. We believe that Jesus died for our sins and that if we confess them and truly turn from them, intending to lead the new life which He offers, then we are cleansed, set free with a completely clean sheet. Every time we fail, we need to return to the cross, so to speak, and claim both forgiveness and restored fellowship. Hopefully, as we continue on the journey with Him, our failures become less and less frequent – a process theologians term 'sanctification'.

We come now to a matter on which Christians disagree – the role of the Holy Spirit. Some claim that when we are born again – that is, we accept Christ as Saviour and Lord – we receive the Holy Spirit in all His fullness; others say that there are two stages: 1) being born of the Spirit and 2) being filled with the Spirit. I belong to the latter group, but it distresses me when Christians separate because of this difference in understanding, so let me explain in greater detail what I believe and why.

First, there is no division into first- and second-class Christians. All who confess Jesus as Lord belong to Him and have been born again of the Holy Spirit; they have eternal life:

> Therefore I want you to know that no one who is speaking by the Spirit of God says, 'Jesus be cursed,' and no one can say, 'Jesus is Lord,' except by the Holy Spirit.
> *1 Corinthians 12:3*

Secondly, although I believe that being filled with or baptised in the Holy Spirit (the descriptions relate to the same thing) is a separate experience, there need be no delay. After Jesus ascended to His Father, the disciples had to wait for the Holy Spirit to come. Having come, He has not departed, and so it is possible for people to be born of the Spirit and filled with the Spirit at the same time. However, in my experience that rarely happens. Perhaps it is because little teaching is given in many churches (and, it seems, in many theological colleges) about the Holy Spirit.

Thirdly, baptism in the Spirit is not a reward for super Christians; He is given to enable weak Christians to fulfil God's plans for them. What is more, we need to go on being filled with the Holy Spirit. On being asked why this was necessary, one believer replied, 'Because I leak.' I find that amusing but misleading; the intention is that the Holy Spirit should be an ongoing stream flowing through us to accomplish the purposes of God in the world.

We have seen that, although Jesus was born of, or conceived by, the Holy Spirit (so He did not need to be born *again*), He had no power to fulfil His ministry until the Holy Spirit came upon Him at His baptism in the form of a dove. Immediately after that he began His ministry. If Jesus is the perfect man – man as God intended all human beings should be, male and female – why should we be different? We have been born again of the Spirit to be clean vessels like Jesus – 'A body you prepared for me ... I come to do your will, O God' (Hebrews 10:5-7) – so we, like Him, have to be filled with the Spirit if we are to receive power. It was a two-stage experience for Jesus, to be born of and then filled with the Spirit. So it is with us – we are born again of the Spirit and then filled with the Spirit for service.

Jesus specifically told His followers to ask the Father to give them the Holy Spirit:

> If you then, though you are evil, know how to give good gifts to your children, how much more will your Father in heaven give the Holy Spirit to those who ask him!
> *Luke 11:13*

I do not understand how that can be equated with repenting, nor with confessing our sins and accepting Jesus as our Saviour and Lord; it is a different and additional instruction and, for me, a different and additional experience. Some Christians, who do not believe that to be filled with the Spirit is different from being born again of the Spirit, argue that I am mistaken in claiming this second experience. I find that frustrating; to me it is similar to an unbeliever arguing with *them* that, because God does not exist, it is impossible for them to have been born again of the Spirit. They know that they have been, although they cannot prove it. In the same way, I know that something happened to me when I asked the Father to fill me with His Holy Spirit.

Why are some Christians, who do not share my understanding, so zealous in seeking to make me deny what I know I have experienced? After all, I have simply followed the instructions of Jesus on this matter. If they choose not to ask, I find it difficult to understand why, but let us agree to differ. It is far more important to preserve the unity of the Spirit; otherwise we both grieve Him.

The fruit and the gifts

Scripture differentiates between the fruit of the Spirit and the gifts of the Spirit. The former has a profound effect on the life of the individual involved, changing the person they are. Paul lists the fruit as love, joy, peace, forbearance, kindness, goodness, faithfulness, gentleness and self-control (Galatians 5:22-23). Notice that he uses 'fruit' in the singular – that is to say, the intention is not that each of us exhibits different fruits but that the whole fruit with all nine attributes is to be expressed through each of us. It is the outworking of the process of sanctification whereby we become more and more like Christ.

The gifts of the spirit are given to the Church for the common good. Paul lists some of them in 1 Corinthians 12:7-11 and others in Romans 12:6-8, but I do not believe these lists are exhaustive. Some of the gifts are dramatic, such as healings or miracles; others less so. Personally, I believe the gift of encouragement to be one of the most beautiful and effective of all. In my experience as a pastor, I have come across so many people who believe that they are a disappointment to others, particularly their parents. It costs so little to say to someone, 'Well done.' Over a period, such encouragement can transform a life.

Unlike the fruit of the Spirit, the gifts are distributed across a church fellowship, as the Holy Spirit decides, with each person having just one or two and no one having them all. This is why it is so important for the individuals to work together as a community if the whole is to function properly as God intends. Unlike the fruit of the Spirit, the gifts do not necessarily have an effect on those who use them. A person with the gift of healing may themselves suffer some disability. The one with a word of knowledge may not have the wisdom to know what to do with it.

If we had to choose between the fruit and the gifts, I would say that the fruit is the more important because in the age to come there will be no need for the gifts. No need for healings – everyone will be well; or for words of knowledge – we shall know even as we are known; but the fruit affects the person we are, the person who goes forward to the age to come. Fortunately, however, we do not have to choose: both the fruit and the gifts are available through the Holy Spirit. However, I do believe we need to guard against concentrating on the gifts, which can appear more sensational than the quieter and deeper work of the fruit. Let me illustrate this with the following story.

I know of a church that had had a worthy ministry in the past but which had lost its zeal, mainly because the leadership had grown older and older and blocked any move on the part of younger members to seek how the Spirit might be leading for the future. Reluctantly, two of the members left the fellowship and set up a new one, seeking to be open to whatever the Lord might want of them. Over time, and this was comparatively brief, they attracted others and numbers grew sufficiently for them to purchase and renovate their own premises. Through prayer and obedience, the fellowship grew to become one of the leading churches in the area with a wonderful outreach to the poor and vulnerable.

Some time later, a church based in a neighbouring town, which had discovered anew the gifts of the Spirit, decided to share their enthusiastic faith by planting a congregation not too far away from this other, now not so new, church. I commend them for their desire to share what they had experienced, but I believe they could have shown a little more wisdom in researching what God was already doing in the area and consulting with leaders of the local churches who were working closely together. Be that as it may, because the manifestation of the gifts of the Spirit was very obvious and dramatic, the numbers at the new church increased rapidly.

Unfortunately, this growth was not so much through new believers as by attracting members from other fellowships – including, and particularly, from the other 'new' church I have mentioned. The growth was so great that there were not enough chairs to accommodate all who attended. At the same time, because so many of their members had transferred to the new church, the other church now had more chairs than they needed, so they offered them as a free gift to the new fellowship.

I believe that generous and selfless act to be a vivid illustration of the work of the Holy Spirit in producing His fruit. To round off the story, I would mention that, 20 years later, both churches are continuing their work. The first has grown again, is continuing its powerful witness and has a high reputation for its work amongst the vulnerable. The other, under new and perhaps wiser leadership, has a more rounded and less sensational ministry but still attracts many who do not feel at home in more traditional churches.

Before leaving the subject, I feel I need to comment on manifestations which, on occasion, seem to accompany the baptism in the Spirit, such as extreme shaking, jumping up and down or making strange noises. I am by no means convinced that they are all genuine manifestations of the Spirit, although it does seem that many people do gently collapse to the ground (described rather dramatically as being 'slain in the Spirit') – something I have never experienced personally. I am strongly influenced by a statement that Paul makes in discussing the work of the Holy Spirit:

The spirits of prophets are subject to the control of prophets. For God is not a God of disorder but of peace.
1 Corinthians 14:32-33

This follows on from his instructions about speaking in tongues in public, as to when this should be permitted and when the would-be speaker should keep silent. Paul is absolutely clear that the person exercising the gifts of the Spirit is not overwhelmed by the Spirit but remains firmly in control of him or herself. The excuse, 'I couldn't help it [whatever it may be]; the Spirit forced me to do it,' is totally invalid. Furthermore, the claim by some Christian groups that unless a person can speak in tongues they have not been baptised in the Spirit is an arbitrary, man-made assessment and has no foundation in Scripture.

I am aware that in referring to speaking in tongues and prophecy I am raising issues that may be outside the experience of many Christians, but I must resist the desire to develop the discussion further lest I become diverted from the main thrust of this book. There are many books on the subject for those who are interested in pursuing these matters further.

The work of the Holy Spirit

We must return to the question of the significance of the work of the Holy Spirit who was given to the Church at Pentecost. What does this mean for us today? Well, first and foremost I have become a child of God:

> Yet to all who did receive him, to those who believed in his name, he gave the right to become children of God.
> *John 1:12*

I have a double assurance of that fact – first the statement of Scripture quoted above and secondly I have the witness of the Holy Spirit within me:

> The Spirit you received does not make you slaves, so that you live in fear again; rather, the Spirit you receive brought about your adoption to sonship. And by him we cry, *'Abba,*

Father.' The Spirit himself testifies with our spirit that we are God's children.
Romans 8:15-16

The Holy Spirit within me confirms to my spirit (part of who I am) that God really is my heavenly Father. It is difficult for anyone to convey to another an experience he or she has had. Conversely, it is easy for someone who has not had that experience to doubt or even deny its reality. Paul doesn't waste time arguing about it; he states what to him is true, and he leaves it to others whether or not they choose to believe him. I can say only that I recognise what he is talking about. The relationship which God originally intended between humankind and Himself has been restored; He has someone else to love who loves Him in return. Often I fail to be what He created me to be (He and I are still working on that) but He is my Father and I am His child. I am no longer under law; I am in a relationship.

Such a remark is often misunderstood and prompts the question as to whether I am free to break the law. It is the wrong question because there isn't a law to break. Now, when I sin – and I am sorry to say I still do – I do not break God's law; I break His heart, and I assure you that I find that far more difficult to live with than breaking an inanimate law. I have disappointed and hurt someone who trusted me, who expected more from me than that, and I feel wretched until I have told Him how very sorry I am and ask His forgiveness. Make no mistake, it isn't easier to live free of the law but in a relationship; it is far more demanding.

I would stress the fact that in saying there isn't a law to break, I am referring to my relationship with my heavenly Father; of course, I am not free to break the law of the land. In nations where there is no law, or where the law is not upheld, there can be neither justice nor righteousness.

Paul gives a vivid description of the work of the Holy Spirit:

> When you believed, you were marked in him with a seal, the promised Holy Spirit, who is a deposit guaranteeing our inheritance until the redemption of those who are God's possession – to the praise of his glory.
> *Ephesians 1:13-14*

When we order an expensive item, we may be asked for a deposit to guarantee our intention to complete the purchase. If the item is on show, a notice reading 'sold' will be attached to it. When we accept Christ as Saviour and Lord, the Holy Spirit is God's notice reading 'mine'. Incidentally, in modern Greek the word behind 'deposit' means an engagement ring. We are to be the bride of Christ!

It is a matter of sadness to me that so many good and faithful Christians believe in their heads that they are God's child but it doesn't seem to have reached their hearts. Some years ago I visited Australia and I was taken into the mountains above Sydney to see the dam and reservoir which store the city's water supply.

We stopped for coffee at a hotel which still exhibits the hydro equipment in use when it was a health spa early in the twentieth century. My hostess told me that her parents had stayed in that hotel for their honeymoon. Apparently her mother had originally been her father's secretary. At breakfast on their first morning she accidentally knocked over a cup and spilled coffee over her new husband. In her consternation, she grabbed a napkin to mop it up saying, 'Oh Mr Smith, I'm so sorry, I'm so sorry.' She knew in her head that she was his wife, but she hadn't yet really accepted the fact that she was no longer his employee. The almighty creator of the universe, the one who one day will judge every human being, is my heavenly Father and I am His deeply loved child. It is true, it is true, it is true.

So the coming of the Holy Spirit fulfils the first purpose of the Holy Trinity in creating us – God has someone else to love. He also fulfils the second – to provide stewards of God's creation, to take dominion over it and ensure that His will is done. Of course, the situation is no longer as it was when God first created all things and He declared that they were very good. Humankind's rebellion affected not only our own relationship with God but that of the whole created order.

> The creation waits in eager expectation for the children of God to be revealed. For the creation was subjected to frustration, not by its own choice, but by the will of the one who subjected it, in hope that the creation itself will be liberated from its bondage to decay and brought into the freedom and glory of the children of God.
> *Romans 8:19-21*

Living the kingdom life

This world is alienated from God, and it is now the task of the faithful to bring in the kingdom of heaven on earth. Ultimately, of course, only God Himself can do that; there will be a time when He cries, 'Enough!' and He will establish His rule on earth as it is in heaven. In the meantime, we who know Him must challenge everything that works against that rule.

I use the word 'challenge' deliberately, but that must not be interpreted as implying violence. Jesus challenged the status quo of His time but did not use violence. Where He found wrong He did all He could to set it right. Where there was sickness He brought healing, where there was hunger He provided food and, on at least three occasions, where there was death He restored life. When faced with injustice, greed and pride He fearlessly pointed it out, but He took no physical action to enforce the justice God demands. Rather He left His words to work within those who heard them. In the end, He provoked such hostility that He was seized and tried on trumped-up charges and sentenced to death.

He proclaimed the truth but did not seek to impose it by force. Rather, He suffered injustice in the belief that in the end truth will prevail. Finally He submitted to death, trusting that His Father would raise Him to life. We are called to follow that same path, not seeking to justify ourselves but leaving it to the Father to reveal the truth we have dared to proclaim and thus provide our justification.

Having said that, there are two further things to consider. I said that Jesus did not use violence, but what about the time He cleansed the Temple? He took a whip and drove out both the cattle and the money changers. First, I would suggest that He used the whip only on the cattle – the normal way to control them – but without cruelty, and not on the human beings. This was not an action directed towards the world; this was the area within the world where God dwelt – the Temple. This was where the holiness and righteousness of God was to be demonstrated to the world, but the priests had desecrated it by turning it into a greedy and corrupt commercial business. It was not the judgement of God on the present world order – that lies in the future – this was His judgement on those claiming to represent Him to the world.

The second point to make is that Jesus did indeed set us an example, but He was a lone individual without the responsibility of government or family. What of a man facing an intruder in his home who threatens to attack his wife and children? Is he to say, 'Jesus offered no resistance and so, as a follower of Him, I must do the same'? I do not believe that. Similarly, a government cannot allow another nation to invade its territory and rape and pillage; nor can it allow any of its citizens to attack or rob its other citizens. Paul is quite clear about that:

> For rulers hold no terror for those who do right, but for those who do wrong. Do you want to be free from fear of the one in authority? Then do what is right and you will be commended. For the one in authority is God's servant for your good. But if you do wrong, be afraid, for rulers do not bear the sword for no reason. They are God's servants, agents of wrath to bring punishment on the wrongdoer.
> *Romans 13:3-4*

I have already said that whilst my relationship with God does not depend on law, that does not mean I am free to break the law of the land. The rule of law is necessary and good and, if it is to be effective, it must be enforced. Scripture explains the situation well:

> If you suffer, it should not be as a murderer or thief or any other kind of criminal, or even as a meddler. However, if you suffer as a Christian, do not be ashamed, but praise God that you bear that name. For it is time for judgment to begin with God's household; and if it begins with us, what will the outcome be for those who do not obey the gospel of God?
> *1 Peter 4:15-17*

The sacraments

Baptism

Different denominations hold different views on how many sacraments there are, but almost all agree on two; baptism and Holy Communion. A sacrament has been defined as 'an outward and visible sign of an inward and spiritual grace[7] – that is to say, acting on the specific instructions of Christ, we do something using material elements (water, and bread and wine) and which can be seen, and God honours this by effecting something in the person involved which is real but spiritual and unseen.

A problem arises over just what it is that God does. It is interesting that, although He gave clear instructions that we should perform these actions, Christ gave little explanation of their effect. Because the grace is inward and spiritual, it is unseen, and all sorts of speculative ideas have been claimed as true. Personally, I think that some claim too little and others claim too much, but we need to be careful because, once again, our different views can cause serious disagreements which inevitably disrupt the unity of the Spirit that is so essential to the Church. The very fact that Christ did not elaborate should cause us to be wary of seeking to force our own views on others. As we administer the sacraments, the actions we perform in the environment of this world are honoured in the eternal kingdom of heaven.

I believe that it was Colin Buchanan, one time Bishop of Woolwich and an authority on liturgy, who pointed out that the New Testament refers to baptism in a number of different contexts and suggests that everything involved in being a Christian is summed up in baptism. Because we are all different, different aspects of what happens will assume greater or lesser importance according to our view or our need. However, just about everyone agrees that it signifies joining the faithful company of all believers. It is a commissioning for service.

Our particular view of what happens will strongly influence our attitude to infant baptism. This is not the place to set out in detail the arguments for and against the practice.

---

[7] A Catechism, *Book of Common Prayer* (1662).

The more emphasis we place on what *God* does in baptism, the more likely we are to accept infant baptism; the more we emphasise *our response* to God's offer of salvation, the more we will opt for believer's baptism – i.e., the person being baptised must be of an age to have personal belief.

On one occasion, a Baptist Minister handed me a small booklet entitled, *What the Bible says about Infant Baptism.* Opening it, I found it to be completely blank. I like to think he did it with his tongue in his cheek rather than seeking a confrontation. It is dangerous to base any argument on silence but, if anything, the absence of any instruction is an argument *for* infant baptism rather than against it. The covenant sign under the Old Testament dispensation was circumcision of male babies on the eighth day after birth, when they were far too young to understand anything of its significance. If the covenant sign under the New Testament was *not* to be administered to babies, you would expect a clear instruction to that effect, noting the change of custom.

Having said that, it is clear that in the New Testament adult baptism is the norm. It is understandable that it wouldn't be long before believing families would ask, 'What about our children? Are they in or out?' This prompts the question, 'In or out of what?' Let us be clear that we are not saved by baptism; we are saved by our faith in the work of Christ on the cross. The Salvation Army does not practise baptism of children or adults but, although I don't understand why they ignore such a specific command of Christ, I do not for a moment doubt their salvation.

So if baptism does not bring salvation, what does it do? It brings us into the new covenant of God, just as circumcision brought Jewish males into the old covenant. In our culture, we place so much (perhaps too much) emphasis upon the individual; the Bible places much more upon the corporate or collective idea of families, tribes and nations.

Rather than set out various theories of baptism, let me share what it means to me. I had the enormous privilege of having Christian parents, which meant that I was brought up in a household of faith. Rather than having to come to faith, to change I would have had to reject the faith I had. Of course, I still needed to make a commitment to accept Christ as my personal Lord and Saviour, but that was a stage – an important and life-changing stage – of a continuous journey which had begun at my baptism as a baby, when God brought me into His promises. Looking back, I can trace His faithfulness in bringing His plans for me to fruition. All my days, in spite of my failures, I have been within His covenant. Of course, I recognise that not everyone baptised as a baby will be saved, but we also need to acknowledge that not everyone baptised as a believer continues in the faith.

It is understandable that when those who are baptised as an infant come to a personal faith, they should be given the opportunity to affirm that faith publicly. The Anglican Church provides that opportunity in the service of Confirmation. When I went through a course of instruction prior to my own Confirmation, I was taught that it was linked in some way (I never quite grasped what the link was) to the coming of the Holy Spirit on the disciples on the Day of Pentecost. I am delighted that this teaching reflects my own view that being filled with the Spirit is a separate event or experience from being born again of the Spirit, but I can find no biblical authority for the claim that Confirmation represents the baptism in the Holy Spirit. In fact, the service of Confirmation is not mentioned in Scripture, and perhaps the link to Pentecost is an attempt to justify it. Recently, the Church of England has provided a liturgy for the Affirmation of Baptismal Faith. In practice, however, this does not seem to provide what some believers who were baptised as infants are seeking. Not only do they want to express the vows for themselves (rather than through godparents making them on their behalf), but they also want to undergo baptism (usually by total immersion).

On the few occasions when a member of our congregation asked about the possibility of being rebaptised, I would share my own view and experience that my baptism as an infant was effective. God had taken the initiative and brought me within His covenant without waiting until I could understand, and I had simply fulfilled or entered into its benefit. However, if they found that they really could not believe that then, rather than letting them be burdened with doubt about the efficacy of their baptism, I would support them in their decision to be baptised by immersion, although, in conscience, I could not perform it myself.

Before leaving the subject, I would share one concern. On one occasion, two members of our congregation had been invited by a friend to witness his baptism in a nearby Pentecostal church. Immediately following the baptism of their friend and one or two other members of that congregation, the pastor asked if there were any present who had committed their lives to Jesus and who would like to be baptised by immersion. The two members from our church took up the offer and were duly baptised (I don't know the details of what clothing and towels were provided), and shortly afterwards they came to tell me in great excitement what had happened.

It so happened that the pastor and I were both members of a local fraternal of Christian ministers, and I raised the matter with him, expressing my concern. He was obviously embarrassed but explained that he did not believe that infant baptism was effective and that adult baptism by immersion was very important and should be offered to all true believers; for him it was a vital matter of conscience. I pointed out that the two people concerned were members of our church and I was their pastor; therefore God would hold me responsible for their care and not him. He should have allowed me to discuss the matter with them rather than going ahead without first consulting me. So that he would understand, I used a biblical analogy and explained that what he had done was to take two of my sheep, baptise them according to his personal beliefs and then put them back in my flock to be cared for. I think the reality of what he had done struck home and we were able to continue in fellowship.

I mention the incident because it illustrates so vividly how important it is that, however strongly we may believe our understanding is right, we preserve the unity of the Spirit in the bond of peace.

Holy Communion

Let me now turn to the sacrament of Holy Communion. Jesus said, 'Do this in remembrance of me' (Luke 22:19). For some that means no more than to recall the fact. On the last night before He was crucified, Jesus gave His disciples bread, saying that it was His body given for them and that the wine was His blood shed for them. Obviously He was referring to His death which He would suffer the next day. So it was to be an opportunity to recall the fact that Jesus gave His life so that we might be forgiven. We already know that, but the Lord's Supper, which is another name for the sacrament, is a specific event to recall the facts. It is calling to mind a wonderful past event. This view is often referred to as a 'low' understanding.

In addition, it is an opportunity for all who are present to do it together – it is a corporate experience; it is COMmunion. That is to say, it happens with others. It so happens, although I know of no specific reason for it, that those who lean towards this simple view of the sacrament usually have individual cups or glasses of wine and they will wait until everyone has one and then they will drink the wine together. I say wine, but very often in such assemblies it is blackcurrant cordial or nonalcoholic grape juice. All drinking together certainly enhances the sense of being the *community* of believers, even if it isn't what happened when the Lord instituted the sacrament.

The next approach I will mention is the other extreme and is a very 'high' view of Holy Communion; in fact, those who hold it will usually refer to it as the 'Mass'. This is the description used most frequently by the Catholic wing of the Church, both Roman and Anglican. In this view we have what is known as transubstantiation – the doctrine that the bread and wine become, at the moment of consecration, in substance, the body and blood of Jesus Christ. Jesus said, 'This *is* my body' and 'This *is* my blood' (Matthew 26:26, 28, italics added); He did not say it *represents* my body and blood. Obviously the bread and wine do not change in appearance, but those who hold this view believe that the act of consecration does effect a real change. It cannot be detected by any scientific method, but nevertheless it really happens. If you are tempted to dismiss this view out of hand, be careful. Do you believe in the human soul or the human spirit? They cannot be detected scientifically but I believe they exist.

So in this high view we are not just remembering what Jesus did at that last supper; He is actually present now in the bread and wine – His real presence. We really do feed on Him. Of course, it isn't in a cannibalistic sense but we do take Christ into ourselves.

You will understand that there is a tremendous difference in the value attached to this sacrament according to whether we see it as the Lord's Supper or the Mass. For one, it is simply calling to mind something that Jesus did; for the other, it is an active participation in the living Lord. For the former, the service of Holy Communion may be comparatively infrequent – perhaps once a month or even, in some Christian communities, once a year on Maundy Thursday. For the latter, the Mass must be a daily or certainly a weekly means of meeting with Jesus and receiving His life into ourselves.

The high view carries with it a corollary. If Jesus is really present in the bread and the wine, if you keep or reserve some of the consecrated elements and put them in a box called a tabernacle or small cupboard called an aumbry, you have the real presence of Jesus before you. In Catholic churches there will be a light burning just above the tabernacle to show that the consecrated elements are there. You will understand that if the real presence of Christ is there it will be venerated, and you will see worshippers genuflect as they pass.

It is for this reason that the 39 Articles, which set out the beliefs of the Church of England, specifically forbid that the elements should be reserved and worshipped in any way. This is why it is laid down that any bread and wine which remain after everyone has communicated are to be consumed by the priest. Having said that, during the Victorian era, what is known as the Oxford Movement within the Church of England reintroduced the high doctrine and Anglo-Catholics today do reserve the sacrament and place it in an aumbry.

There has also been another change over recent years. Very often I am asked to consecrate extra bread and wine so that during the week an authorised lay minister such as a Reader may take Communion to the sick. With the shortage of clergy, this is happening more and more frequently. Indeed, during an interregnum (that is, while there is a vacancy in a parish), the bishop may authorise occasional services of Communion by extension where a Reader will conduct a service of Holy Communion using elements consecrated by a priest in advance. However, there is no question of the elements being worshipped or venerated because, it is believed, no transubstantiation has taken place.

So that brings us to the generally accepted view of the Church of England. It won't surprise you to learn that it is middle of the road – somewhere between the low and the high views. We do more than recall to mind what Jesus did and we do less than believe that there is a material change in the bread and wine. We do believe in the real presence of Jesus, but not in the Catholic sense; rather in a similar manner to the promise of Jesus that states, 'For where two or three gather in my name, there am I with them' (Matthew 18:20). We treat the consecrated bread and wine with respect because they have been set apart for a holy purpose, and we don't pour any unused consecrated wine back into the bottle.

Don't take this analogy too far, but think what happens when we buy a house. There is a deed of conveyance. It is a tremendously important document because it really does convey the building to us; it is our proof of ownership. But we don't live in the document; we live in the house. The bread and wine are tremendously important, but we are *united* with the living Lord Jesus.

We take the words, 'Do this in remembrance of me,' very seriously. That is to say, we do more than recall to mind what Jesus did. Think of it this way: if someone says to you, 'I have remembered you in my will', you would be somewhat miffed if, when they die and the will is read out, it simply says, 'I remember Bill and the happy days we had together'; you expect something more tangible. So it is when we remember Jesus in Holy Communion. Jesus is the host in two senses. We remember indeed that He is the victim who died for us, and the bread and the wine represent His body and blood given for us in His death and so we receive the benefit of that death. In the words of the service just before we come to receive, 'Draw near with faith ... remember that He died for you.' We receive into ourselves the benefit of His death – the forgiveness of sins and acceptance into the family of God. But He is also the host in the sense that, no matter who actually gives us the bread and wine, we are receiving it from Jesus Himself. He is present with us even if we do not see Him, because it is His table.

I should mention one other aspect which is associated with the service. Many churches have the custom of the bread and wine being brought up the aisle by two members of the congregation, usually at the time that the collection of money is brought up. Very often, extra words are inserted that refer to the fact that we are offering bread and wine and that we receive them back as the body and blood of Jesus. This is a symbol that we can offer everything we do to the Lord and that He can transform it in His service. It is true that we should be able to offer everything we do to the Lord for Him to use, but personally I find this an intrusion into what happens at Holy Communion. In this service, above all, the emphasis is on what Jesus did for us, not on what we do for Him. Only at the end of the service, after we have received the bread and wine, do we offer Him our souls and bodies to be sent out to work for His praise and glory.

The Church of England does not spell out in great detail what happens, or how it happens, in Holy Communion, and I am grateful for that because it is not always possible to define a spiritual experience. Nevertheless, *something* happens; it isn't just a memory. From all that I have said, you will understand that this service means different things to different people. As I explained before, we are all different and God relates to each of us on an individual and personal basis, and we need to be careful before we tell someone that they are wrong to believe this or that about what Holy Communion means. So let me explain what Holy Communion means to me. Please take from it what you find helpful and leave what you don't.

I was brought up in an evangelical church that tended towards the lower view of Holy Communion, but, even so, that was still much more than just calling to mind what Jesus did. I was taught that the central truth of the Communion service was that Jesus had died for my sins. The bread was broken, as His body had been on the cross; the wine was poured out, as His blood had been by the nails, and I received the benefit of that sacrifice. My sins were forgiven and I had eternal life. That was the limit of the meaning of Holy Communion and I must not try to add more to it.

However, over the years I have met with other Christians who hold different views, and I have come to see the service in a richer light. It is true that in the broken bread and poured-out wine Jesus was clearly referring to His death, and so, of course, we remember that and receive the benefit of it – that lies at the heart of the service. However, when Paul describes the institution of Holy Communion, which he claims he received as a direct revelation from the Lord, he explains that Jesus said, 'Do this in remembrance of *me'*, not just 'in remembrance of my death'.

In addition, this is Matthew's description of what happened:

> Then he took a cup, and when he had given thanks, he gave it to them, saying, 'Drink from it, all of you. This is my blood of the covenant, which is poured out for many for the forgiveness of sins. I tell you, I will not drink from this fruit of the vine from now on until that day when I drink it new with you in my Father's kingdom.'
> *Matthew 26:27-29*

Even as He was handing them the wine and referring to His blood being poured out, Jesus was thinking ahead to what His death would accomplish – to the future when the kingdom will be set up on earth as it is in heaven and all who believe in Him will reign with Him. If Jesus was looking ahead to the future, why shouldn't we?

The kingdom of heaven really does exist now; Jesus is on the throne at the right hand of God the Father. It is so very near; we may not be able to see it with our eyes but the veil which separates us is very thin. When I come to Holy Communion, it isn't simply to receive the bread and wine; it is the whole action of drawing near with faith. The veil between this world and the next is somehow pierced and I touch eternity. I don't need to believe that the elements are transubstantiated into the body and blood of Jesus; the bread and wine, meaningful as they are, I receive from Jesus Himself. And there is more: I am united with that great company of faithful believers who are worshipping Him just the other side of the veil as we are worshipping Him on this, and as we shall do together when the kingdom of God is fully come. I believe that among their number is my wife, together with other loved ones who have gone ahead of me, and that is a comfort, although that thought is secondary because central for both them and me is Jesus Himself.

To me, Holy Communion is so much more than calling to mind something Jesus did on the last night He spent on earth. As I say, it is here that I touch eternity, the kingdom that is coming on earth as it already is in heaven.

Chapter 7
What happens then?

The only thing in life of which we can be absolutely certain is that it will end, yet we do so little to prepare for what will happen next. For those who believe that this life is all there is and that nothing happens next, that is understandable, but for those of us who believe that there is life after death and that that life, being eternal, is even more important than this, it is astonishing. Of course, we can excuse ourselves by claiming that we do not know in any detail what that life will be and so there is nothing we can do to prepare for it other than commit ourselves to Jesus and trust Him to see us through. Ultimately that is true, but there is the danger that what we do not know we may invent, and all sorts of weird and wonderful theories abound. Where did the idea come from that we will sit on clouds in white robes playing a harp?

Scripture may not supply us with details – probably because they would be meaningless to us in our present state of limited understanding – but there are some very clear pointers which most preachers seem to ignore. Have you ever heard a sermon on 'What happens when we die?'? I have heard only one, and that was because I was preaching it! I am not thinking of the many I have heard about being raised to eternal life; I have heard quite a number of those (thanks be to God), but few about what that life will involve.

I have done some research on the subject but, whilst there is a considerable amount of wild speculation, it is not easy to find reliable and well-reasoned information. I will share what I have discovered but, for obvious reasons, it is not based on personal experience.

In the Old Testament there is little understanding of life after death. There is the phrase, that so and so lived or reigned for this number of years and then he 'slept' or 'rested with his ancestors' (e.g., 1 Kings 2:10). The place of the departed is called *Sheol* and is a place of shadows where the soul is in a state of limbo. At one time it seems that the Jews believed that *Sheol* existed as a place or power independent of God, but later they saw it as being within His dominion, although those who were there were unaware of, or cut off from, His covenant. However, you will remember the words of the psalmist in that great Psalm 139:

> Where can I go from your Spirit? Where can I flee from your presence? If I go up to the heavens, you are there; if I make my bed in the depths [the Hebrew word is *Sheol*], you are there.
> *Psalm 139:7-8*

I am sure the psalmist is right: we believe God created everything, so how can there be any place where God is not?

At the time Jesus walked the earth, the Pharisees believed that there was life after death and the Sadducees did not. When Paul was on trial before the Sanhedrin (the Jewish court), in the course of his defence he very cleverly claimed that he was on trial because of his belief in the resurrection. This immediately got the Pharisees and the Sadducees arguing against each other about whether or not there *was* a resurrection and it stopped the trial, at least on that occasion (Acts 23:6).

We need to remember that Scripture teaches that Jesus was the first to rise from the dead (Acts 26:23). This is the great victory of Easter. Even though the Pharisees believed that there would be a resurrection, no one had actually experienced it. So where were the dead until then? Scripture says that they were held in 'Hades' (which is the New

Testament word basically equivalent to the Old Testament *Sheol*) by or at the instigation of Satan (e.g., Proverbs 5:5; Psalm 116:3). Because all have sinned, Satan was able to say to God, in effect, 'By your own decree, no sinner is able to enter heaven; but because everyone has sinned they all belong to me.'

Jesus seemed to develop this understanding of Hades and *Sheol* (although He was only building on something the Jews were themselves coming to believe) – that it was divided into two: one part for the righteous and one part for the unrighteous. He told the story of the rich man and the poor beggar named Lazarus who sat at his gate. Jesus explains:

> The time came when the beggar died and the angels carried him to Abraham's side. The rich man also died and was buried. In Hades, where he was in torment, he looked up and saw Abraham far away, with Lazarus by his side. So he called to him, 'Father Abraham, have pity on me and send Lazarus to dip the tip of his finger in water and cool my tongue, because I am in agony in this fire.' But Abraham replied, 'Son, remember that in your lifetime you received your good things, while Lazarus received bad things, but now he is comforted here and you are in agony. And besides all this, between us and you a great chasm has been set in place, so that those who want to go from here to you cannot, nor can anyone cross over from there to us.'
> *Luke 16:22-26*

We must be careful because this is only a story Jesus told to illustrate a point. The characters – Lazarus and the rich man – were not necessarily real people who had lived. But Jesus could not be referring to the final state of heaven because He had not yet died and risen and, as we have seen, He was the first to rise from the dead. So there is a strong hint that within *Sheol* or Hades there was a place of some sort of torment or deprivation and a separate place for the righteous, who were still held captive because of sin, but it was not unpleasant. This was the paradise to which Jesus referred when He told the thief on the adjoining cross, 'Today you will be with me in paradise' (Luke 23:43).

Actually, there is another difficulty here. Hades is simply the place of the departed; it is not normally thought of as the place of torment – that is a different word, *Gehenna*, where the fires are continually burning. The implication is that the wicked are sent there only after the final judgment (Matthew 10:28).

The problem is that in English both *Hades* and *Gehenna* are translated by the same word: 'hell'. There is another difficulty also. As human beings confined at present to this life, we have to think in terms of time, and God is not bound by time. This must make a great difference to our present comprehension. But obviously Jesus was seeking to convey *some* truth meaningful to us living out our lives here on earth, and certainly in this parable of Lazarus and the rich man He does seem to speak of a division within Hades.

But let us return to the general point that everyone who died was held captive to Satan in some way because everyone who died was a sinner. Do you remember that great vision that John describes in the book of Revelation of the risen Christ who says to him:

I am the First and the Last. I am the Living One; I was dead, and now look, I am alive for ever and ever! And I hold the keys of death and Hades.
Revelation 1:17-18

Isn't that wonderful? We have that great picture of the risen and ascended Jesus towering above John saying, 'Look, I have the keys of the prison of death.' In the words of the Te Deum, 'He has opened the kingdom of heaven to all believers.'

It seems that the biblical picture is that, until the resurrection of Jesus, all who died went to a place named *Sheol* or *Hades*. When Jesus died He went to paradise which apparently is part of *Hades*. He also went to what is described as *Tartarus*. The word appears only once in the New Testament (2 Peter 2:4). To add to the confusion, this is also translated as 'hell'. Scripture does not say that any human beings went to *Tartarus* but rather fallen angels. Peter records that Jesus went to preach to the fallen spirits.

> For Christ also suffered once for sins, the righteous for the unrighteous, to bring you to God. He was put to death in the body but made alive in the Spirit. After being made alive, he went and made proclamation to the imprisoned spirits — to those who were disobedient long ago when God waited patiently in the days of Noah while the ark was being built.
> *1 Peter 3:18-20*

I have already explained that 'made proclamation' does not mean to evangelise; it means to proclaim, as the above translation correctly states. Jesus was not seeking to evangelise and win these fallen angels; He went to tell them the battle was over. They, as servants of Satan, had lost and he, Jesus, was victorious. Notice also that it says that Jesus was made alive *in the Spirit* – that is to say, He had not yet risen from the tomb and so He did not have His resurrection body. This has importance regarding something I will explain a little later.

So what is the situation now? Well, it seems that when we who believe in Jesus die, we go straight to be with Him. Unlike those of the Old Testament, we do not go to *Hades*. The cross and the resurrection are so powerful and so effective that the situation has been totally changed.

However, that does not mean that we will immediately enter the final state of heaven. Paul writes to the Thessalonian Christians:

> According to the Lord's word, we tell you that we who are still alive, who are left until the coming of the Lord, will certainly not precede those who have fallen asleep.
> *1 Thessalonians 4:15*

There is another verse to put alongside that. It comes in the letter to the Hebrews where the writer has been going through a list of Old Testament characters who remained faithful throughout their lives. He says, 'so that only together with us would they be made perfect' (Heb 11:40). Those who have already died will not go into the final state of heaven without us, and those alive when Christ returns will not go ahead of those who have died.

It seems that what Scripture is teaching is that all those who have gone ahead of us in faith have already entered into the closer presence of Christ – they are with Him, and we will go to join Him with them – but the final state of glory, the fullness of the kingdom of Heaven, is something we all enter together. I love that thought: no one gets there first; all believers in Jesus get there together with Him. In my imagination (and you must not take this picture too literally) I see all those who have died in faith gathered with Jesus outside some great and wonderful place and asking excitedly, 'Can we go in now?' and Jesus is joining in the joy and excitement but saying, 'Not just yet; there are still some more to come.' Finally, when all the elect are gathered together, Jesus cries out, 'Right, in we go...' and we all go in together.

It has to do with the time when Jesus will have put down all rebellion and when the last enemy – death – has finally been destroyed. At present, death, like Satan himself, has been defeated but not destroyed. Paul says:

Then the end will come when, he [Jesus] hands over the kingdom to God the Father ... When he has done this, then the Son himself will be made subject to him who put everything under him, so that God may be all in all.
1 Corinthians 15:24, 28

As I have already explained, eternal life is not the same as everlasting life. Everlasting life could be no more than this life going on and on for ever and ever. I don't know about you; I love this life, but I certainly don't relish the idea of it never coming to an end. I hope for something better than this. Eternal life refers to quality not quantity. It *is* everlasting because it is the life of God Himself in us and He is eternal, but it is a new quality of life, far superior to this.

And because it is eternal it exists now – it wouldn't be eternal if it didn't begin until after death, would it? We enter eternal life in this life here on earth. Jesus said:

Very truly I tell you, whoever hears my word and believes him who sent me has eternal life and will not be judged but has crossed over from death to life.
John 5:24

If you have made Jesus your Lord and Saviour, you already have eternal life because His life is in you. More than this, Jesus Himself is in you and He is eternal, so of course you have eternal life.

Allow me to share with you something I discovered fairly recently – certainly during the years since I retired. Jesus said, 'Very truly I tell you, whoever obeys my word will never see death' (John 8:51).

There are a number of Greek words which the Bible translates by our verb 'to see'. The Jews who hear Jesus say this take it literally to mean that such a person would never die, and they use it as evidence that Jesus must be demon possessed. However, the particular word Jesus uses here means 'to notice particularly'. Do you remember on Easter Sunday how the two disciples run to the tomb? John gets there first and 'sees' that it is empty (John 20:3-5). The Greek word translated there as 'see' implies a glance. But when Peter arrives, he goes into the tomb and he 'sees' (it is a different word in the original) that the bandages round the head are separate from the bandages round the body – he *particularly notices* that. The word 'see' here is the same one – 'to notice particularly'.

It seems that what Jesus may be saying is that those who, in this life, love Him and keep His word will not particularly notice death. We will be busy living this life with Him and serving Him and it will be one of those occasions when it seems that He is particularly close. For me, those occasions are all too rare and I wish they lasted longer. Perhaps it happens when you are lost in worship, or something has happened when you need Him particularly and His presence is very real. On this occasion, you will realise that He has never been quite so real, and you will be busy enjoying Him more than you have ever enjoyed Him before and then it will suddenly occur to you – 'Good gracious, I must have died and I didn't notice it.' Isn't that lovely? If we belong to Jesus now, we will not particularly notice death.

Eternal torment?

Now I want to change tack briefly and talk not about heaven but about hell. Will those who reject the salvation of Jesus live for ever in torment?

Let me explain first of all that the mainstream teaching of the Church, or certainly the Church of England and the evangelical wing in particular, is (or has been) that the human soul is indestructible and that the enemies of God are destined for everlasting fire. However, although I was taught it, I have come to reject that view. Let me explain why and then you can make up your own mind.

Let me remind you of a verse I have already quoted: when Adam sinned God drove him out of the Garden of Eden saying:

> The man has now become like one of us, knowing good and evil. He must not be allowed to reach out his hand and take also from the tree of life and eat, and live for ever.
> *Genesis 3:22*

God expressly prevents man from living for ever in His fallen state. That seems to me to be pretty conclusive, and I do not understand how many, perhaps most, evangelicals, who set such store by the truth of Scripture, can claim that unredeemed humankind will live for ever, let alone that it will be in torment in hell.

Secondly, there is the statement in Paul's first letter to Timothy: 'God, the blessed and only Ruler, the King of kings and Lord of lords *who alone is immortal*' (1 Timothy 6:15-16, italics added). So, if God alone is immortal, surely that means that, unless a person is in God, he or she does not have immortality, so they *cannot* live for ever.

How, then, has the belief arisen that unbelievers will be tormented in hell for ever? It must be the references in Scripture to them suffering eternal punishment. So let me deal with those verses and try to reconcile them with the statement that man is not immortal.

'Then they will go away to eternal punishment, but the righteous to eternal life' (Matthew 25:46). These are the words of Christ Himself. Most commentators hold that the biblical phrase 'eternal life' means much more than existing for ever and ever. It has to do with a new quality of life. So either the meaning of 'eternal' in 'eternal punishment' is used in a different sense and does mean only 'existing for ever', or it refers to some sort of punishment we do not readily understand.

When discussing penal substitution, I referred to the phrase 'capital punishment' to describe the death penalty. If (as 1 Corinthians 15:24 quoted above states) all rebellion against God will be destroyed, then the punishment Jesus is referring to is death. However, what we call death is not eternal. Christians believe that everyone will be raised to face judgement, albeit that Christians will not be condemned because they are in Christ. Those who will not submit to God will then be annihilated. *That* death or destruction *will* be eternal. Hence it is eternal punishment, and that is what Christ is referring to here to distinguish it from the first death which we will all experience (unless Christ returns beforehand).

> He will punish those who do not know God and do not obey the gospel of our Lord Jesus. They will be punished with everlasting destruction and shut out from the presence of the Lord.
> *2 Thessalonians 1:8-9*

The word behind 'destruction' is *olethros* from *olethreu* which means 'to slay'. Here the clear statement of destruction is linked to the word 'everlasting' and would appear to support my interpretation of Matthew 25:46 above.

'They serve as an example of those who suffer the punishment of eternal fire' (Jude 7). I suggest that this has led to confusing the fire and the torment. Let me explain. I have said already that in the Bible we have translated two words as 'hell'. One is *Hades* which, as we have seen, refers to the place of the departed before Christ's resurrection, and the other is *Gehenna*, which is 'hell fire'.

The implication of this becomes clear when we understand that just outside Jerusalem is the valley of Gehinnom, which at the time of Jesus was the local rubbish tip. Here the fires were kept burning continually. All the waste rubbish of the city was thrown into it and was burned up. The fires never went out, but any particular *piece* of rubbish was totally destroyed – *that* piece did not go on burning for ever. By speaking of *Gehenna*, Scripture is linking it to the valley of Gehinnom.

To me, the picture is clear: all the rubbish of society – that which is unfit to dwell in the eternity of heaven – will be cast into the all-consuming wrath of God. That is to say, the fire of the wrath of God is eternally set against anything that would disturb the perfect eternal harmony of heaven, but in the consummation of all things there will be nothing to suffer that wrath because it will have been destroyed.

A third angel followed them and said in a loud voice: 'If anyone worships the beast and its image and receives its mark on their forehead or on their hand, they, too, will drink of the wine of God's fury, which has been poured full strength into the cup of his wrath. They will be tormented with burning sulphur in the presence of the holy angels and of the Lamb. And the smoke of their torment will rise for ever and ever. There will be no rest day or night for those who worship the beast and its image, or for anyone who receives the mark of its name.'
Revelation 14:9-11

This highly figurative description is indeed difficult to explain, but notice it is the smoke of the torment that rises for ever. Think of the towers of the World Trade Centre in Manhattan. A month after the attack, television pictures showed that the smoke was still rising, even though, sadly, the people had long since perished.

We need to be careful not to take the descriptions in the book of Revelation too literally; they are intended to convey a general truth. For instance, in Revelation 4 we are given a picture of 24 elders sitting on thrones. Four living creatures cry out, 'Holy, holy, holy is the Lord God Almighty…' Whenever they do so, the 24 elders fall down before Him who sits on the throne, lay their crowns before Him and utter their own hymn of praise. But we are told that the four living creatures never stop praising Him. So when do the 24 elders get back to sitting on their thrones?

Obviously we are not intended to ask such literal questions. This passage about torment is intended to convey the fact that those who will not accept the rule of God will face some terrible punishment. I suggest we are not intended to press the details.

> Then I saw a great white throne and him who was seated on it. The earth and the heavens fled from his presence, and there was no place for them. And I saw the dead, great and small, standing before the throne, and books were opened. Another book was opened, which is the book of life. The dead were judged according to what they had done as recorded in the books. The sea gave up the dead that were in it, and death and Hades gave up the dead that were in them, and each person was judged according to what they had done. Then death and Hades were thrown into the lake of fire. The lake of fire is the second death. Anyone whose name was not found written in the book of life was thrown into the lake of fire.
> *Revelation 20:11-15*

What I have just said about the book of Revelation applies to this passage also, and I would add this. As we have seen, what we call death is not permanent; we will all rise to be judged. Faithful believers will enter the kingdom and rule with Christ. Those whose names are not written in the book of life will be thrown into the lake of fire, which is 'the second death' (v. 14). I suggest that the second death is the real one, and it is annihilation which is indeed eternal. Finally, *Hades* is thrown into the lake of fire along with death (v. 14) and is itself destroyed.

This is the reason why I believe, based on the words of Scripture, that unbelievers will not suffer eternal torment. Some will disagree with me, of course, but I would ask that they consider the texts I have quoted which indicate that the human soul is not immortal and offer an explanation as to why, nevertheless, they believe that it is. I would add also that, for me, in my understanding of the Father I have come to know through Jesus, I cannot conceive that He would allow that there should be anything anywhere throughout eternity in rebellion against Him and suffering torment. Scripture says that God is to be all in all, so how can anything exist in eternity where God is not?

Now I have explained all that, please do not misunderstand what I am saying. I do not believe everyone will be saved; I do believe that hell exists and that, sadly, some people will end up there. Scripture refers to hell far too frequently to dismiss it, but I do not believe anyone or anything will exist in torment *for ever*. They will have been annihilated. I am delighted to discover that more and more Christians seem to be coming to that conclusion.

But to return to what happens to believers. We will retain our individuality. As Paul explains in 1 Corinthians 15:35-54, here we have an earthly body which is perfectly suited to life in our present environment; we don't go floating off the earth into outer space. So we will have a new spiritual body, perfectly suited to the life of heaven.

However, it does seem that there will be a different way of recognising each other. We have already considered the number of occasions when the risen Jesus was not recognised. Mary did not recognise Him at the tomb until He spoke her name. The two on the road to Emmaus did not realise it was Jesus until they invited Him into the house to eat, and they recognised Him when He broke the bread.

Have you ever wondered what we will look like in heaven? My grandmother died when I was about six; she knew me only as a little boy. My ten grandchildren know me only as an old man. How will both my grandmother and my grandchildren recognise me when we are all together in heaven? I don't know, but I am sure that we *will* recognise each other because we will still be individuals with our own personalities.

Let me stress the fact that we will not be disembodied spirits floating around. If you look in 2 Corinthians 5, you will see that Paul clearly states that he doesn't want to be spirit only; he wants to have a new body through which he can express himself. It will be a body perfectly adapted to our new environment of the kingdom of Heaven just as our present bodies are adapted perfectly to our present environment. What is more, our future bodies will be related in some meaningful way to our existing bodies, which will be transformed. The resurrection body of Jesus still bore the marks of the nails and the spear; no longer suffering wounds but signs of His victory and glory. It seems that we do not receive our resurrection bodies immediately when we die – although, as I say, we shall go to be with Christ – but we all receive them together when we go with Christ into the new heavens and earth. That will be the promised resurrection of all things.

There is another thing I must point out, and I hope it will not distress you. In heaven we shall not be married. Some people, even Christians, seem to think that the life to come is no more than this life continued in glorious technicolour. In fact, it is a totally different quality of life where Jesus will be the very centre of our being.

Forgive me if I share something very personal, but it may help you to understand. Shortly after my wife died, a friend said to me, 'There is something I think you would like to know. You may remember that I visited you both about a month before Sheila died. You happened to be out of the room and she and I were chatting when she said, "I love Ken and the family dearly, but I cannot wait to be with Jesus.'" She died suddenly and unexpectedly of a heart attack four weeks later. I am so glad that my friend shared that with me; it is so encouraging. That is how we ought to be – in a deeply loving relationship with each other, but with Jesus as the centre of our lives. The bottom line is that God made us for Himself, not for each other.

We cannot, any of us, choose the manner of our death (unless we commit suicide, which is not an option), but it seems to me to be a tremendously exciting adventure. When I am dying, if it is possible, I intend to be looking for Jesus who, I believe, will be there to greet me. With Him, I believe, there will be many of my friends and loved ones, all waiting to welcome me. Maybe amongst them will be the child we lost in a miscarriage (I am not quite sure about that); if so, that will be so very exciting – meeting a child I never knew. Of course, Sheila will be there. Just what our relationship will be I do not know. Somehow it is going to depend on our relationship with Him for whom to live is life and to die is gain. Sheila and I and all those I love will share in the glory of the Lamb and we shall say to each other, in whatever language or means of communication we have in heaven, 'Isn't He wonderful!'

The final consummation

So far I have described what Scripture seems to be pointing to immediately after death – we go to be with Christ – but that is not the final state. For that we have to wait until all the elect are gathered in and we will all enter the resurrection life together. Here I must acknowledge my debt to Bishop Tom Wright and, in particular, his book *Surprised by Hope*.[8] I am not holding him responsible for everything I share because he set me thinking, and it has now become part of me with my slant

[8] Tom Wright, *Surprised by Hope* (SPCK, 2007).

on it. I will deliberately refer to texts I have already quoted and add to what I have said.

First let me remind you of that strange text in Matthew:

> And when Jesus had cried out again in a loud voice, he gave up his spirit. At that moment the curtain of the temple was torn in two from top to bottom. The earth shook, the rocks split and the tombs broke open. The bodies of many holy people who had died were raised to life. They came out of the tombs after Jesus' resurrection and went into the holy city and appeared to many people.
> *Matthew 27:50-53*

Let us notice two things about that: first, it was only holy people who were raised – I take that to mean the faithful under the Old Covenant – and, secondly, it was only after Jesus had *risen* that they were seen. The Bible is clear that Jesus was the first to rise from the dead, and so Scripture is consistent.

Then there is the text from Revelation where the risen Christ tells John:

> I was dead, and now look, I am alive for ever and ever! And I hold the keys of death and Hades.
> *Revelation 1:18*

Everyone who has ever lived, with the exception of Jesus Himself, has sinned. Scripture says, 'The one who sins is the one who will die' (Ezekiel 18:20). So everyone was held in death, and here is the Lord appearing after His great victory of the cross and resurrection saying, 'I hold the keys of death and Hades', and He has released the righteous from their prison.

We saw that Paul was convinced that when he died he would go to be with Christ:

For to me, to live is Christ and to die is gain. If I am to go on living in the body, this will mean fruitful labour for me. Yet what shall I choose? I do not know! I am torn between the two: I desire to depart and *be with Christ*, which is better by far.

Philippians 1:21-23, italics added

I suggest that Paul knew he would be aware of that fact; he is hardly likely to say that state would be far better if he were literally asleep or unconscious. However, let me stress, Scripture is speaking of those who are in Christ; there is no hint about what happens to those who do not believe. I don't know what happens to unbelievers when they die but I don't need to know. Scripture concentrates on those who have been saved.

Before I move on, let me deal with one problem that may occur to you. If Christ was the first to rise from the dead, how was it that when Jesus and some of His disciples were on the Mount of Transfiguration Elijah and Moses appeared with Him? Well, there is no difficulty about Elijah: you will remember that Elisha saw him being taken up into heaven (2 Kings 2:11-12). Elijah didn't die and so he didn't have to rise from the dead; but Moses did die. However, there is something very strange about his death. Scripture says that *God* buried him (Deuteronomy 34:6). Now what does that mean? It is so obscure that several modern translations simply say, 'He was buried', without stating by whom. Moffat is more definite and translates it as 'The Eternal buried him'. Let's put that statement alongside something in the little quoted letter of Jude:

But even the archangel Michael, when he was disputing with the devil about the body of Moses, did not himself dare to condemn him for slander but said, 'The Lord rebuke you!'

Jude 9

Apparently Satan had an argument with the archangel Michael regarding the body of Moses. I suggest that it was about the fact that Moses was a sinner and he had died and so, like everyone else, he should go to *Sheol* or *Hades*. But because we are told that God Himself had buried Moses, God chose to do something different with him, and that is why he was able to appear with Elijah on the Mount of Transfiguration. Again, isn't it wonderful how consistent the Bible is?

It seems that Paul uses the term 'asleep' to convey the fact that the Christian dead are alive and aware but, not having their resurrection bodies, they are not fully complete. You will recall that when Jesus went to the spirits in *Tartarus* after He had died, but before He rose in His resurrection body, Scripture says He had been made alive in the spirit. It seems that that will be our state initially: alive in the spirit but not with our resurrection bodies.

There is a passage in Revelation which relates to this:

When he opened the fifth seal, I saw under the altar the souls of those who had been slain because of the word of God and the testimony they had maintained. They called out in a loud voice, 'How long, Sovereign Lord, holy and true, until you judge the inhabitants of the earth and avenge our blood?' Then each of them was given a white robe, and they were told to wait a little longer, until the full number of their fellow servants, their brothers and sisters, were killed just as they had been.
Revelation 6:9-11

I have already spoken of imagining all the dead who were believers waiting in excitement asking, 'Can we go in now?' Here it is not quite like that, but this passage refers specifically to those who have been martyred and who are calling for God to destroy all those who have attacked the Lord's people. However, it does add weight to the idea that these martyrs are conscious and with the Lord, even though they do not have their resurrection bodies.

Just to complete my argument, let me quote from the first letter to the Corinthians:

> Listen, I tell you a mystery: We will not all sleep, but we will all be changed – in a flash, in the twinkling of an eye, at the last trumpet. For the trumpet will sound, the dead will be raised imperishable, and we will be changed. For the perishable must clothe itself with the imperishable, and the mortal with immortality.
> *1 Corinthians 15:51-53*

So let me recap. When we who belong to Christ die, we go to be with Him, but that is not the time of resurrection. We wait until God decides that the time has come and then Jesus will return, bringing with Him all who belong to Him, and those who are still alive on the earth will be raised up to meet Him. Then all of us will be given our resurrection bodies – imperishable ones.

But what then? What will we be doing in eternity? Well, we do not know in detail but Scripture gives lots of clues, and we need to put them together to get some idea of what the situation will be.

First of all we must grasp a wonderful truth. It isn't only human beings who will share in the resurrection; the whole of creation will be involved. Look again at this from Romans 8:

> The creation waits in eager expectation for the children of God to be revealed. For the creation was subjected to frustration, not by its own choice, but by the will of the one who subjected it, in hope that the creation itself will be liberated from its bondage to decay and brought into the freedom and glory of the children of God. We know that

the whole creation has been groaning as in the pains of childbirth right up to the present time.
Romans 8:19-22

Do you understand what that is saying? All creation is waiting for the time when all who believe in Jesus will be revealed as God's children – that is, when Jesus returns and we are changed and made complete with our imperishable bodies. At that time, creation itself will be released from its bondage to decay.

That was from Paul. This is Peter:

As you look forward to the day of God and speed its coming. That day will bring about the destruction of the heavens by fire, and the elements will melt in the heat. But in keeping with his promise we are looking forward to a new heaven and a new earth, where righteousness dwells.
2 Peter 3:12-13

Just as our bodies are to be changed into resurrection bodies which will not be subject to pain, suffering or death, so there is to be a new heaven and a new earth which will not be subject to decay. And just as Christ's resurrection body was not an entirely new creation (that is to say, His original body was not left behind in the tomb), but was His earthly body *transformed* into a body perfectly suited to a different environment, so our bodies and also the new earth will reflect a continuity with our present bodies and the present creation.

What will we be doing? We shall be ruling over the new earth where everything works as God originally planned. I wonder if that disappoints you. Perhaps you have believed that you would be released from earth and would dwell with Jesus in heaven. Well, you will dwell with Jesus in heaven, because the kingdom of Heaven will have come on earth. Every time you pray the Lord's Prayer you are asking 'Your kingdom come on earth as it is in heaven.' Do you mean it? Do you believe that one day that will happen? At the resurrection of all things that *is* what will happen. Listen to this from the book of Revelation:

> The seventh angel sounded his trumpet, and there were loud voices in heaven, which said: 'The kingdom of the world has become the kingdom of our Lord and of his Messiah, and he will reign for ever and ever.'
> *Revelation 11:15*

Heaven and earth will be united because both will be the kingdom of God.

What do you want to do in eternity? In the future we won't be idle, like some people in retirement who have no interests and gradually fade away; we shall be active, helping our Lord rule over an earth which works perfectly. The curse God put upon the ground when He told Adam:

> Through painful toil you will eat food from it all the days of your life. It will produce thorns and thistles for you ... By the sweat of your brow you will eat your food.
> *Genesis 3:17-19*

will not be carried into the new earth; work will be the joy that God originally intended – cooperating with Him in ruling over His creation.

Now do you understand what Jesus was getting at when He told the parable of the faithful servant who made use of his talents:

> Well done, good and faithful servant! You have been faithful with a few things; I will put you in charge of many things. Come and share your master's happiness!
> *Matthew 25:21*

The reward for serving Christ well in this life on this earth will be to be given greater responsibility and opportunity to serve Him on the new earth in the resurrection of all things. What is more, the actual works you perform for Jesus in this life will survive in some way. Listen to what Paul tells the Corinthians:

> For no one can lay any foundation other than the one already laid, which is Jesus Christ. If anyone builds on this foundation using gold, silver, costly stones, wood, hay or straw, their work will be shown for what it is, because the Day will bring it to light. It will be revealed with fire, and the fire will test the quality of each person's work. If what has been built survives, the builder will receive a reward. If it is burned up, the builder will suffer loss but yet will be saved – even though only as one escaping through the flames.
> *1 Corinthians 3:11-15*

Later in the same letter Paul sums it up by saying:

> Therefore, my dear brothers and sisters, stand firm. Let nothing move you. Always give yourselves fully to the work of the Lord, because you know that your labour in the Lord is not in vain.
> *1 Corinthians 15:58*

In the resurrection, the work you have done for the Lord in this life will survive in some way and be made manifest in the new earth.

When we understand that there is to be a new resurrected earth, it makes sense of some Old Testament prophecies, such as:

> The wolf and the lamb will feed together, and the lion will eat straw like the ox, and dust will be the serpent's food.

156

They will neither harm nor destroy on all my holy mountain,' says the LORD.

Isaiah 65:25

How can such a prophecy be fulfilled unless there *is* a new earth in the eternal kingdom of heaven? Remember that Jesus said, 'Blessed are the meek for they will inherit...' what? Some vague benefit up in the air? No, they will inherit the earth (Matthew 5:5).

And think of the wonderful description at the end of the book of Revelation:

Then I saw 'a new heaven and a new earth,' for the first heaven and the first earth had passed away, and there was no longer any sea. I saw the Holy City, the new Jerusalem, coming down out of heaven from God, prepared as a bride beautifully dressed for her husband. And I heard a loud voice from the throne saying, 'Look! God's dwelling-place is now among the people, and he will dwell with them. They will be his people, and God himself will be with them and be their God.'

Revelation 21:1-3

I did not see a temple in the city, because the Lord God Almighty and the Lamb are its temple. The city does not need the sun or the moon to shine on it, for the glory of God gives it light, and the Lamb is its lamp. The nations will walk by its light, and the kings of the earth will bring their splendour into it.

Revelation 21:22-24

However much symbolism there is in Revelation, it is clear that the new Jerusalem comes down from heaven to *earth*. It isn't that we go to dwell with God but He comes to dwell with us. The effect may be the same, but the wording highlights the fact that we take up our appointed role on earth together with

Him; and the kings of the earth bring their splendour to the Holy City.

What about that passage in 1 Thessalonians which speaks of those who are alive being caught up in the air when Christ comes again? Doesn't that imply that they will *leave* the earth?

> For the Lord himself will come down from heaven, with a loud command, with the voice of the archangel and with the trumpet call of God, and the dead in Christ will rise first. After that, we who are still alive and are left will be caught up together with them in the clouds to meet the Lord in the air. And so we will be with the Lord forever.
> *1 Thessalonians 4:16-17*

Do you remember the description in the Gospels of the triumphal entry of Jesus into Jerusalem, riding on a donkey? The writers describe two crowds. There were those who had come to the Passover from Galilee, who had seen Jesus work great miracles and had heard His teaching, and they joined Him rejoicing as He entered the city. Then there were others who had come from distant lands, perhaps like Simon of Cyrene, making a once-in-a-lifetime journey to the Passover. They didn't know who Jesus was, and they asked what all the fuss was about. But John tells of a third crowd:

> The next day the great crowd that had come for the festival heard that Jesus was on his way to Jerusalem. They took palm branches and went out to meet him, shouting, 'Hosanna!' 'Blessed is he who comes in the name of the Lord!' 'Blessed is the king of Israel!'
> *John 12:12-13*

These were people who had already arrived in Jerusalem for the feast and who knew about Jesus and, hearing that He was on His way, they went out of the city to greet Him and welcome Him.

When Jesus comes, bringing with Him all the faithful who have already died, those believers who are still alive at the time will rise up in the air to welcome Him and lead Him not into some distant heaven but to the new earth where He is to rule as King, and where they will be with Him for ever.

So the situation is that when we die, we who believe in Jesus and have made Him our Lord and Saviour go to be with Him. But that is not the resurrection. We wait until the time is fulfilled that God has already laid down. Then, everyone and everything that does not accept the sovereignty of God will be destroyed. Jesus will come with all the faithful who have died, while the faithful who are still alive on this earth will be raised up to greet Him and welcome Him. It is then that we will all receive our resurrection bodies which will be perfectly suited to the new earth which will come down from heaven and which will work perfectly, with no weeds and no earthquakes. Like us, it will be a new creation, and we will take up the role which God always intended we should have – to rule over the earth together with Jesus, acting as the stewards of God.

The acts we have done on this incomplete, imperfect earth which have been done for Him will survive and form part of the new creation. How important it is, therefore, that we devote our energies now to building the kingdom of God, to doing all we can to abolish poverty and want, unfairness, violence and corruption, and to bring peace and joy wherever we can. The parable of the talents, where the servants of the master put those talents to work so that they have something to give Him when he returns, is not just a story to encourage us to do good; it really is part of bringing in the kingdom, and that work will survive and be part of the new earth where we reign with Jesus, and God is all in all.

The story is nearly complete. As we have just seen, God's purpose for man to be His steward on earth and care for it will be fulfilled. But what of the other reason for our creation – the desire of the Godhead to have someone else to share in His love? That also is wonderfully fulfilled:

Then I heard what sounded like a great multitude, like the roar of rushing waters and like loud peals of thunder, shouting: 'Hallelujah! For the Lord God Almighty reigns. Let us rejoice and be glad and give him glory! *For the wedding of the Lamb has come, and his bride has made herself ready.* Fine linen, bright and clean, was given her to wear.' (Fine linen stands for the righteous acts of God's holy people.)
Revelation 19:6-8, italics added

And look again at the passage from Revelation that I quoted earlier:

I saw the Holy City, the new Jerusalem, coming down out of heaven from God, prepared as a bride beautifully dressed for her husband. And I heard a loud voice from the throne saying, 'Look! God's dwelling-place is now among the people, and he will dwell with them. They will be his people, and God himself will be with them and be their God.'
Revelation 21:2-3

The Holy City, which is the bride, the wife of the Lamb (Revelation 21:9), is, of course, populated by those who already belong to Christ – that is, the Church. Paul more than hints at that intimate relationship in his letter to the Ephesians:

Husbands, love your wives, just as Christ loved the church and gave himself up for her to make her holy, cleansing her by the washing with water through the word, and to present her to himself as a radiant church, without stain or wrinkle or any other blemish, but holy and blameless.
Ephesians 5:25-27

The plan of God to make man in His own image, capable of giving and receiving love and sharing in the life of God the Trinity, will be fulfilled. The Church, the faithful company of all believers, becomes the bride of Christ – a picture of the close intimacy which will exist between Christ and us. The plan was set out in the opening chapters of Genesis and, in many books written by many authors at different times, all inspired by the Holy Spirit, we read the continuous story of how God wooed a rebellious people – us – back to Himself, patiently leading us at the pace we were willing and able to travel in our understanding of who He is and what He desires. The plan is fulfilled in the closing chapters of Revelation. As I have said, it is a love story – the greatest love story there can ever be. It isn't yet quite complete, but it is certain and sure.

Chapter 8
My Lord and my God

This chapter is a sort of postscript because I have already set out in some detail the stage I have reached in my understanding of God. I have been greatly helped on my journey by hearing the experiences of others further along the road than I. And so, in the hope that it may be of benefit to others, I will share something of how God has brought me to where I am now. It is, of course, deeply personal, and that is dangerous because it can be embarrassing to witness the feelings and emotions of others. But Scripture records the emotions of Jesus and perhaps we – and especially we British – are too reluctant to share ours.

Allow me to repeat what I have already said more than once: we are all different and Christ relates to each of us individually, so do not expect Him to lead you as He has led me. However, I hope you will be encouraged to believe that He desires to have a relationship with you that is truly personal.

The early years

I cannot remember a time when I did not believe in God. Before I was old enough to understand anything, my parents prayed with me every evening when I was put to bed. Presumably they were Christopher Robin prayers because I can just remember the phrase, 'Please God, make me a good boy.' I don't know how effective they were but the mere act of praying instilled in me the fact that God existed. Some might claim that this was indoctrination and that I should have been left to make up my own mind when I was older as to whether or not I would believe in God. That argument can be applied equally to whether or not I should have been taught to clean my teeth. I was free to stop cleaning them later in life, but I was not deprived of the benefit of the practice in the meantime.

I accompanied my parents to church on a regular basis and eventually joined the church choir and the youth group. I remember one Bank Holiday Monday, when I was about 16, going on a ramble with the group, led by the vicar. (Only now do I appreciate his dedication in giving up the opportunity to relax with his family after the hectic period of Holy Week and Easter, with all its extra services.) When we stopped for our picnic lunch he sat next to me, and in the course of conversation he asked, apparently in passing, whether I had ever considered ordination. Actually I had, but I had firmly rejected the idea because I could not face having to take so many services. I told him my decision, but not the reason for it, and thought no more about it.

After completing my National Service in the army, I had no specific career in view and I found myself in the insurance industry, first with Lloyds of London and then at the head office of a leading insurance company. The government was running a campaign to reduce the incidence of tuberculosis in the nation and my company offered all their employees the opportunity to attend a mass X-ray unit during office hours. Most of us took advantage of it, and I attended with a colleague who was a particular friend. At the unit, there was a notice explaining that the X-ray would be taken on 35mm film, and any small defects in the backing material would show up and involve a recall of that person for a full-scale X-ray. Of the whole of our department, only two of us were recalled: my friend and myself.

Another good friend of mine had died of TB some three years earlier, and the disease was known as a killer, so I was very frightened. The delay involved in fixing an appointment for the full X-ray and then an interview to be told the result was not long, but it seemed interminable. Of course, I prayed.

As I began to tell the Lord of my fears and ask that the X-ray should be clear, something happened that I had never before experienced. I am not sure whether it was a voice or a thought, but alongside my own words were those of another. I suppose a sceptic would say the thought came from my subconscious, but now, in the light of further experience, I believe that it came into my mind prompted by the Holy Spirit. It was a question: 'If one of you is to be ill, which of you shall it be?' Immediately I rejected the thought as an intrusion and continued in my prayer; at least I tried to, but again I had an experience I had never had before – my prayers did not get through. I can say only that it was as though they hit the ceiling and never left the room; somehow I was aware that they were blocked.

The next night, again I tried to pray but before I had even started the question came again: 'If one of you is to be ill, which of you shall it be?' Again I rejected it – surely a good God would not want anyone to be ill. So I pressed on – at least, I said the words but, as before, I was keenly aware that the route to God was blocked and my words went nowhere. This continued night after night. Eventually, in desperation and certainly with no hint of generous self-sacrifice, I gave my answer, which I can still remember with perfect clarity: 'Well, if it has to be one of us, I suppose it had better be me because he is married and I am only engaged – but I don't see why it has to be either of us.' It was simple and churlish, but I knew deep within myself that a serious transaction had taken place. If it later transpired that I had the disease, I could not complain; in some way I had committed myself. Immediately, the route for my prayers cleared; I was able to pray freely and I knew I was in touch with God again, and I asked that we should both be well.

Eventually, the two of us were called back to hear the results of our X-rays – he was clear; I had TB. It was active and it was in both lungs.

I was referred to the chest clinic in my local area. The consultant had been appointed very recently, and he was young with his own ideas. He told me that he would not give me any medication for at least six weeks. I was to go to bed where I could read for an hour in the morning and an hour in the evening and listen to the radio for an hour morning and evening, but for the other 20 hours I was to lie there doing nothing. I really cannot remember what I thought about, other than that any plans I had for my life had almost certainly gone; I was by no means sure I would have a life anyway. I realised that I was not in control of anything; my only hope was God.

The waiting list for a place in a sanatorium was about six months so I needed home nursing. The specialist nurse attached to the clinic, in contrast to the consultant, was very near retirement. She was of the old school and for most of her career there had been no effective medication for TB; the only treatment was bed rest and fresh air. She would have seen many of her patients die, so she must have thought it was encouraging to tell me, 'You are not to worry; there is no reason at all why, if you do all that the doctor tells you, in 12 years' time you shouldn't be able to have a gentle game of tennis.' I was 23, so 12 years was more than half my lifetime. I had been sports captain at school and was still playing rugby – the possibility of a gentle game of tennis in the distant future was not a great incentive.

A strange encounter

It was some time over the next few weeks that I had one of the strangest spiritual experiences of my life, although I did not find it particularly dramatic at the time. It was in the course of my usual evening prayers and I was sharing with God my desire to be healed; however, I added, 'But it must be your decision, not mine.' In view of my experience earlier, I was by no means certain that God wanted me well. Suddenly Jesus appeared behind me, over my left shoulder. I must explain that I was kneeling at my bed and my eyes were closed, so I could not have 'seen' Him in the ordinary sense, but there He was. He slowly shook His head from side to side and said, 'You know, what I want for you isn't always the exact opposite of what you want.'

I have noticed that on the comparatively rare occasions over the years when the Lord has spoken to me, He doesn't use the sort of approach or phrases that I might expect. Why didn't He state simply, 'You will be healed'? In fact, of course, the whole experience, words and actions, was far more personal. I certainly took it to mean that I would recover, but it also made me feel that the Lord was taking a personal interest and was on my side. I was fighting only the disease; not God as well.

Owing to a cancellation, I secured a bed at a sanatorium after just over three months. I spent six months there, followed by convalescence at home for a further three; so, in total, I was off work for a year.

Over the next four years I married my wonderfully supportive fiancée and we bought our first home. When we had just received the news that we were to have a baby, following one of my regular check-ups I was told that the TB had flared up again in one lung. Medication had improved and, although treatment still involved bed rest, I returned to work after just six months. It was a stark reminder, which perhaps I needed, that I was not in control of my life; I was dependent on God.

My wife and I attended our parish church reasonably frequently until my sister-in-law told us that she had joined a church a little further away which was throbbing with life. She suggested that we should try it out; we did and were hooked. The secret of its success, as so often is the case, was that the Bible was faithfully preached and expounded week by week. Looking back, I realise that it had been equally faithfully preached in the church where I had belonged to the choir and youth group, but perhaps my time, or rather God's time, had not yet come.

Over the next few months, my wife and I grew spiritually at an astonishing rate. In view of the faith we had already, I suppose it was that the seed fell on fertile ground. We committed our lives to God as a conscious and deliberate act. Had I not done that already? If I had been asked that question at the time I think I would have said yes, but only in the somewhat negative sense that, having TB, I had had no alternative. Now it was a positive offering of myself; I belonged to the Lord and would follow where He led. Within a year my wife had been appointed an assistant leader of the Women's Fellowship (which had more than 300 members) and I was in charge of the Children's Church.

A few months later the vicar announced that he was moving to another parish many miles away. On his last Sunday in the parish, we arranged that I would attend church in the morning but would stay at home with our young daughter in the evening, because the vicar's wife had asked all her assistant leaders to sit with her at her husband's final service. During the afternoon, my mother telephoned to say she had just remembered that it was our vicar's farewell and would we like her to come and babysit that evening? So I was able to go with my wife, although, of course, we kept to the original plan that she sat with the vicar's wife while I found a seat where I could in the packed church.

The vicar took as the text for his sermon, 'I thank Christ Jesus our Lord ... that he considered me trustworthy, appointing me to his service' (1 Timothy 1:12). He spoke of the wonder, joy and privilege of the work of a parish priest, and explained that he had been working in the insurance industry when God had called him to full-time service in the ministry. In trying to explain later to a questioner the effect it had had on me, I said it was as though someone had thrown a brick which had hit me in the back of the neck. I heard no voice, but I knew God had called me to ordination.

I spent our bus journey home wondering how I should break it to my wife. When my mother had left and we were sitting at the table having supper, my wife asked me what I had thought of the sermon. With much trepidation I replied, 'Well, I think the Lord wants me to be ordained.' With far less concern she said, 'O, I am so glad; He told me, too.'

I am sorry to say that, in spite of that confirmation, I did all I could to avoid the call. I really did not want to be a clergyman. At the time, it was my practice to begin my daily appointment with the Lord by reading from 'Daily Light'. It is a compilation of biblical texts set out for each morning and evening of the year. At the head of the page is a text followed by others which develop its theme. The next morning I read, 'Brethren, give diligence to make your calling and election sure.' That hit me like a blow to the stomach, but I wouldn't give in; I was struggling with trying to follow the Lord but, at the same time, resisting the call.

Two days later I read, 'Thou hast a little strength, and hast kept my word, and hast not denied my name.' I wasn't sure whether I was denying His name but I was certainly denying His call. Then I thought of a good excuse: my father's first wife had died tragically young, and when he married my mother he was 30 years older than she was. I told the Lord that he was likely to die long before her and I would have to do what I could to care for her. That evening I read, 'There is no man that hath left house or brethren, or sisters, or father, or mother, or wife, or children, or lands, for my sake, and the gospels but he shall receive ...'

So that was that argument gone, but I had another. I had a wife and child to support and we were buying our house. Clergy pay, especially a curate's, was notoriously low; it would be irresponsible for me to give up my current job. The next morning I read, 'Go ye ... into the vineyard, and whatsoever is right I will give you.'

By the Saturday night I felt terrible; I was torn apart trying to do what I wanted but knowing that God wanted something else. I sent my wife to bed, saying I would be up shortly, and knelt at a chair. I told the Lord that I would give in and offer for ordination but that I would be a terrible priest because I so didn't want to be one and He would have to do something if I was to be of any use. The next morning I awoke to find that, apart from marrying my wife, I had never desired anything so much as to be ordained. I learned the lesson that the Lord demands obedience first irrespective of personal choice; any benefits may follow later.

In spite of the desire, however, I told myself that I would proceed cautiously and take my time. As our vicar had left, I decided that that morning I would take the opportunity to attend our daughter church which I hadn't visited before. In his sermon, the curate told the story of Gideon who was called by God to serve Him. He put up an argument as to why he couldn't respond, and when that didn't work he tested the Lord by putting out the fleece of a sheep; if in the morning, the fleece was wet with dew but the ground was dry, he would know the call was genuine. That was exactly what happened, but Gideon prevaricated by demanding another test; this time the fleece should be dry and the ground wet. Again it happened. The preacher said that Gideon was wrong to test the Lord when he knew perfectly well what He had commanded, but at least he delayed no longer. Once he was sure that God was with him, he acted!

Let me explain what I believe was happening through all of this. I do not for one moment suggest that when whoever

169

prepared 'Daily Light' was selecting his texts, God directed him to choose the particular ones he decided upon just for me, knowing that sometime in the future I would be reading them on those particular days. Rather, the Holy Spirit, working through my spirit, drew my attention to particular words that were already there. Similarly, the Holy Spirit put it into my mind to go to the daughter church rather than the parish church because He knew He would be able to use the curate's sermon to push me into taking the next step. If the curate had been preaching on a different topic, the Holy Spirit would have found some other way to direct me.

Not a journey; more like an obstacle course

I wrote to The Diocesan Director of Ordinands who was also a suffragan (i.e., deputy or assistant) bishop living at Blackheath – a suburb of London. He gave me an appointment for an evening after work. I got there in good time and sat on a bench beside a church which stands on a corner of the heath. There I opened my copy of 'Daily Light': the words that sprang out at me were, 'Commit thy way unto the LORD; trust also in him; and he shall bring it to pass.' I had to hold on to those words over the next few years because there were difficult obstacles to overcome.

The bishop was pleasant, but as soon as I mentioned my health record the interview was over. He told me that the selection process for clergy involved a medical examination and I would never get through. He thanked me for offering myself for ordination, told me he was sure that I would find ways of serving God as a layman and led me towards the door. I saw all my hopes disintegrating before my eyes and in desperation I said, 'Bishop, if I am wrong about God calling me to ordination, I don't think I can ever again trust that I am hearing Him correctly.'

He stopped and looked at me, and I could almost see the thought forming in his mind, 'I am not going to be the one responsible for destroying this man's faith.' He said, 'Let me tell you what I will do. The diocese has a pre-selection committee which decides who should be sent forward to the selection board of the Church of England. I will put your name down to meet the committee, but please don't be disappointed if they turn you down.' It was obvious that he expected me to fail, but he was giving me the opportunity to discover that for myself.

I returned home with various emotions churning around, predominantly one of anger. That evening, once again, I sent my wife up to bed, knelt at the chair and really let the Lord have it. I reminded Him that I had never wanted to be ordained so why had He pursued me until I capitulated and then given me the intense desire that I should be, if it was never going to happen? Obviously I would fail the medical and no doubt I would be regarded as an invalid for the rest of my life. I was pouring out my hurt and frustration when suddenly He burst in with equal anger. It was a similar experience to the occasion when He asked, 'If one of you is to be ill who should it be?' but this time I was very aware of His 'tone of voice', even though it all took place within my mind, bypassing my ears. He said, 'Look, you have given your life to me. If I say you will be ill, you will be ill; if I say you will be well, you will be well. It has nothing to do with doctors or bishops.'

Reflecting on the experience later, I realised just how wonderful it was that He dealt with me as He did. He might have spoken gently to calm me down, but that wouldn't have had the same effect. He engaged in a real argument. He conveyed His anger that I wasn't trusting Him – especially as He had only that evening given me the text that He would 'bring it to pass' – but the message itself was so wonderfully encouraging. I really did belong to Him; He really had taken control of my life, and the final sentence was almost amusing – the views of doctors and bishops were irrelevant.

Maybe there are some who would say that I was wrong to express my anger to God; He is almighty and I am His creature. Well, maybe I should have been a little more humble, but I wasn't blasphemous and I believe He was delighted. I was treating Him as a reality; someone with whom I could have a true relationship. This was a son complaining to His Father that He had acted unfairly. God could deal with my outburst far more easily than with a false piety.

My appointment with the committee was a lurid example of how such interviews should *not* be conducted. I was called in and given a seat at one end of a long table. Along the sides were at least ten people (every one male!), all of whom seemed to be smoking pipes and with their faces turned to inspect me. At the far end sat the bishop of the diocese (Southwark) and next to him a person I recognised.

The bishop asked the first question: 'Has anyone ever suggested to you that you should be ordained?'

I replied, 'Yes, my Lord,' (such was the way to address bishops in those days) and I pointed to the man on his right who had been my vicar. 'Mr. Wolters, when I was 16.'

To this the bishop commented helpfully, 'Pity you didn't respond then; it would have made it much easier than it is now.' He explained that the church could probably find the money to train me, but there was no money to care for my wife and child while I was at theological college for three years; could my wife go back to work? I had to answer that this was not an option because we had recently discovered that our second child was on the way. This was a further complication.

In the end, it all came down to my appalling health record. Before any further consideration they would send me to have a medical.

The Church of England had – and probably still has – Christian doctors who generously offered their services to the Church free of charge. I was sent to one whose consulting rooms were just off Harley Street. After a careful but brief examination, he put me in front of a sort of living X-ray machine which apparently showed my inside there and then without the need to take a picture. He returned to his desk and asked, 'Which college are you going to?' I explained that we hadn't got that far; the Church authorities were convinced my TB record would mean I would fail the medical. He said, 'Oh, I'm not worried about you; I assume you are having regular check-ups. We would pick you up straight away if anything goes wrong. It's people out there who have no idea of their state of health I'm worried about. You can start training tomorrow as far as I am concerned.'

With the health problem out of the way, the next was finance. I was called to an interview with the secretary of the selection board at Church House, Westminster. He was as helpful as he could be but it rapidly became clear that there was no way that I could provide for my wife and family during the years I would have to spend at theological college. He thanked me for offering for ordination and my papers were filed.

I discovered that older ordinands were sometimes permitted to cut their training to two years instead of three, so my wife and I decided to build up some savings. At £5 a month it was pitifully little, but with two children and the mortgage it was all we could afford on a salary of about £800/900 a year (this was well over 50 years ago). I was working on the principle of the loaves and fishes; if I supplied what I could, maybe the Lord would multiply it. So we continued for the next two years.

On the move

It was early in the summer of 1960 that we read in the newspaper of a scheme proposed by the recently appointed Bishop of Southwark – the one sitting at the far end of that long table had retired. It was headlined as 'A Night-school for Priests'. The Bishop believed that the Lord did not confine His recruitment to the priesthood to those who had just left school. If older people could study for secular degrees through evening lectures arranged by universities, why shouldn't the Church train some of its clergy in the same way?

I wrote for details and applied to join. I learned later that there were 99 applications and, after interview, I was one of 33 who were accepted. The Bishop was determined that no one should be able to say that his protégés were poorly trained and so he asked Kings College, London, to provide the lectures and full examinations. The only concession was that we would be allowed to take the exams in the subjects we had studied each year, rather than having to sit all of them together at the end of the three years. The scheme was given the imaginative name, 'The Southwark Ordination Course'.

The Bishop was anxious to commence the training that September rather than wait until the following academic year, so we began before the great majority of us had passed the official selection process which was completed over the next eight months. This meant that some candidates proved totally unsuitable and were rejected or dropped out along the way. In the end, only 13 of the original 33 were ordained.

The training was intense. We had to attend two lectures a week and initially write 12 essays per term. However, it was soon recognised that this was too demanding and the number of essays was halved. In addition, we had to attend training over one weekend a month and spend two weeks a year at a residential summer school (I was entitled to three weeks holiday), and all this while we continued in full-time employment. I mention these details only to illustrate the pressure and stress it all created for an 'invalid who might be allowed a gentle game of tennis in 12 years' time.' I was in the Lord's hands and my health indeed had nothing to do with doctors or bishops. When I was going my own way, not listening to the Lord, He took away my health. When I listened and obeyed, He restored it.

Immediately before ordination, clergy go into retreat for a few days. This is a withdrawal from the duties and pressures of everyday life. At that time in the Southwark diocese this was held at 'Greyladies' – so named because the lay order of sisters who ran it wore grey uniforms (Southwark was so imaginative). It was situated on the border of Lewisham at the edge of Blackheath. On the Saturday evening before my ordination the next day, I made a short pilgrimage to the far side of the heath to the bench on which I had sat five years earlier when the Lord had given me the text, 'Commit thy way unto the LORD; trust also in him; and he shall bring it to pass.' I thanked Him for His faithfulness in removing the apparently insurmountable obstacles along the way, and bringing it to pass. On my walk back to the house it occurred to me that it was 12 years since I had been sent to bed with TB – I could have a gentle game of tennis!

This is not a biography of my career as a priest but a record of those occasions when the Lord intervened in my life in a particular way. The next was a year later. The custom of the Church of England is to make its clergy deacons, with limited authority for their first year, and ordain them as priests some 12 months later, again preceded by a retreat. In my case it meant I would be away over my birthday.

My wife gave me a copy of a recently published book, *The Cross and the Switchblade*, as a present to take with me (having first surreptitiously read it herself). It is the story of David Wilkerson, a Pentecostal Minister who worked with astonishing success among knife-carrying gangs of youths in the United States, in which the Holy Spirit plays a leading role. I decided I would ask the Lord to fill me with His Spirit.

I knew that during the ordination service the bishop would lay his hands on my head and pray, 'Receive the Holy Ghost for the office and work of a Priest in the Church of God, now committed unto thee by the imposition of our hands.'[9] I had no idea what the bishop thought of the then current renewed interest in the baptism of the Spirit, but that seemed to me to be an appropriate occasion for me to receive it, and I asked the Lord to honour the bishop's prayer. I am not sure what I expected would happen. In fact, it was nothing dramatic; I found that my breathing changed, becoming slower and deeper for a while.

That evening when the excitement of the day was over and the children were in bed, my wife said, 'While you were away I discovered I can speak in tongues' – one of the gifts of the Holy Spirit. I was pleased for her but I remember thinking, 'I'm supposed to be the priest; the bishop laid his hands on *me*.' She, also, had asked the Lord to fill her with His Spirit and He had done so without requiring the services of a bishop. We had always seen my ordination as a joint calling to ministry and I am so pleased that the Lord encouraged her in this way. Within a few days I discovered that I, also, was able to speak in tongues.

Confirming my role

There was another occasion, after I had become vicar of a parish, when I was not so delighted; in fact, I have to admit that I was resentful. My wife was an area leader in the Lydia Prayer Fellowship – a movement where small groups of

---

[9] *The Book of Common Prayer* (1662).

women gather for prayer. What is special about their approach is that they do not come with an agenda but wait, often for a considerable period of time, for the Holy Spirit to lead them to the matters that *He* desires them to pray about. My wife attended a four-day residential conference for Lydia leaders, and on the final evening they gathered for a service of Holy Communion at 8 pm.

The Spirit was present in power and they were caught up in worship until after midnight; they actually heard the sound of 'a mighty rushing wind' (see Acts 2:2). When she returned home, for some while she was a different person; spiritually she was still on the mountain-top. She had had an experience of the Lord far beyond anything I had ever known. I found it very difficult to cope with. I had all the everyday problems of running the parish, but she was on another plane and I could hardly communicate with her. In my heart I knew I should be pleased for her, but my feeling was one of intense resentment. At first I thought it was jealousy, which made me even more annoyed with myself.

Every morning I laid my feelings before the Lord, asking Him to help me deal with them, but I made little progress. It must have been getting on for a week later when I realised what lay at the heart of my problem – I felt inadequate. I was the vicar, the spiritual leader of the parish, but I recognised that I had never been anywhere near what my wife had experienced. How could I lead others (albeit that in this case it was my wife) if they were closer to the Lord than I was?

I poured out my feelings to God. He answered in the rather oblique way I was coming to recognise. 'If I choose to give everyone in the congregation an experience of me beyond anything you have known and to give you nothing, that will not affect by one jot the fact that I have made you their leader.'

That set me free in a way I had not known before. As I saw people in the parish using spiritual gifts which I did not have, I was able to rejoice with them. There were times when good things happened but in which I was not involved in any way; I felt superfluous, but for a long while I had taught that God had given His gifts to every member of the fellowship so that He could use them, and I stood back and watched Him do it.

By gathering together occasions when the Lord has spoken to me directly, it may seem that it has happened frequently, In fact, it has been rare, and then only when He could make known His will in no other way. There is a text which reads:

Whether you turn to the right or to the left, your ears will hear a voice behind you, saying, 'This is the way; walk in it.'
Isaiah 30:21

Some believers take that to mean that God will speak to them frequently – particularly when they have an important decision to make. That isn't so, because in Scripture the Lord's way is always straight; to turn to the left or the right is to go off course. There is no need for Him to correct us if we are walking in the right direction. It is important to understand this if we are to mature into the people He has designed us to be. I learned this lesson in a very practical way.

In the early 1970s, few people owned a freezer. We had a friend who had one and who told us how wonderful it was. My wife thought it might be a way to save money in the long run: to buy food in bulk and in season. However, a freezer was expensive and we felt that it was a luxury we ought not to have. It didn't help that at just that time our curate preached a sermon about the rich fool who decided to pull down his barns to build bigger ones to store more food.

For more than a week I wrestled with the Lord, seeking His guidance. Finally He said (and I was aware of a note of exasperation), 'You know my views about what you do with your money; I don't mind whether you have a freezer or not. You decide!' It wasn't that God wasn't interested; this was a father teaching his son to take responsibility. Scripture says that one day we are to judge angels; we will need some degree of maturity to do that. (Incidentally, we bought the freezer.)

There was another occasion when the Lord taught me an important lesson. Along with most Christians, I can identify with the problem expressed by Paul in his letter to the believers in Rome: 'I do not understand what I do. For what I want to do I do not do, but what I hate I do' (Romans 7:15).

When I was on my knees I really did want to walk with the Lord, but when I rose and engaged in everyday affairs, so often I found myself going in a very different direction. I became frustrated, and one morning I told the Lord, 'I do not want to have free will; it is hindering my walk with you, so I give my free will to you.'

The Lord replied in a very personal way and said, 'Ken, that is lovely and I accept your offer. Now I give it back to you …' (I tried to interrupt with my objection but He continued) '… because I want you to have something to offer me tomorrow.' It is so obvious when we think about it: any relationship of love must involve a continuous act of self-giving; that is what love is.

The closing years

In the year when I was to retire in the autumn, my wife and I were on an early summer holiday in Bulgaria when she had a stroke. Of course, it was a difficult time; she was taken to a hospital more than 20 kilometres away and I was alone in a resort, unable to speak the language. After five days the doctors agreed that she could return to England on a special medical plane. I was not allowed to accompany her but flew back on my original ticket.

When I returned home and while she was recovering in a local hospital, a member of the congregation asked me how I had coped in the crisis; had I felt the Lord particularly near? I had to reply that I had not; in fact, I had not sensed His presence at all. I had been isolated from my fellow beings because of the language barrier, and God did not seem to be there either. For those five days I had to rely solely on my past experience of Him and on what I believed. God had always been faithful in the past and so, irrespective of what I felt, I trusted that He was there and would bring me through that difficult time, which He did.

It seems that all Christians go through periods when we have to hang on by our fingertips. We do not own God; perhaps He needs to remind us of that from time to time.

Although my wife made a wonderful recovery, ten months after my retirement she had an unexpected heart attack early one morning and died. Maybe she made a sound, or perhaps a sudden movement woke me; certainly she was still warm.

We cannot be sure what happens at the moment of death. Those who have had a 'near-death' experience speak of being able to look down on their body and then being drawn back into that body and eventually recovering. Perhaps, therefore, the soul lingers briefly before going on to be with the Lord. (I rather hope that He will be there to meet me when my time comes.) Assuming that she might be aware of me and my actions, I didn't want to cause her regret or sadness. So I knelt at the bed and told the Lord that I handed her willingly to Him.

I must admit that I have little time for Christians who, with what I regard as a false piety, claim that 'death is nothing at all.' I prefer the robust honesty of Paul who describes it as an enemy (1 Corinthians 15:26). Yes, with all that I am I believe in the resurrection life and that death has been defeated by Jesus rising from the tomb. However, whilst it is defeated, it is not yet destroyed.

I remember speaking to a colleague who specialised in bereavement care who told me when he lost his own wife, 'My years of comforting others didn't help at all.' So it was with me; I firmly believed that Sheila was alive with the Lord, but my grief was intense. I was functioning adequately in making arrangements for the funeral and, in contrast to the time the previous year when she had had her stroke, I was aware that God was with me, but I was too churned up inside for Him to have a chance to reveal Himself. She had died on a Saturday and it was on the following Tuesday morning, as I was in the kitchen preparing my breakfast, that He spoke. There was no tenderness and He was abrupt: 'She never belonged to you; she has always been mine.'

It was a shock because it came out of the blue and I wasn't in a time of prayer. I began to say, 'Lord, look after her for me,' when He overrode my words with, 'What do you mean, "Look after her for you"? I let you look after her for me for 42 years.' Set out like that, it seems to have been a conversation, and so it was, but it took no time at all. To speak the words takes just over five seconds, but time was not involved; I was aware of the whole exchange in an instant.

In the course of this book I have repeated several times my belief that God deals with each of us on a personal basis and, because we are all different, we will experience Him in different ways. Even as He spoke, I realised that His brusque manner was exactly what I needed; it was right for me at the time. I could rejoice that Sheila was with her Lord. She had indeed always belonged to Him and He had lent her to me, not simply for my joy – although that was true – but so that I could help her become what He had always planned she should be. What a difference it would make if only every married couple understood that truth.

I haven't yet completed my journey – quite; but I have come so far and it has been so good. The future, I am sure, will be even better.